Advanced Supply Chain Management and Logistics in Agriculture

भाकृअनुप
ICAR
Indian Council of
Agricultural Research (ICAR)

Dr. Balasaheb Sawant Konkan
Krishi Vidyapeeth (DBSKKV)

NAHEP
National Agricultural Higher Education
Project-Institutional Development Plan
(NAHEP-IDP)

nipa
NIPA® Genx Electronic Resources &
Solutions P. Ltd., New Delhi-110 034

About the Authors

Dr. Chandrahauns Chavan is a Senior Professor at Jamnalal Bajaj Institute of Management Studies (JBIMS). University of Mumbai. He is Associated with the institute since 2005. In the year 2006 at the age of 38. he became the Director of the JBIMS & leading for six years for two terms between (2006-09 & 2015-18). Almost eight years he was associated with Ministry of Corporate Affairs, Institute of Company Secretaries of India, Government of India in the capacity of Joint Director and Assistant Director (Academics). He was also holding the additional Charge of Professor cum Director of Alkcsh Dinesh Modi Institute of Management Studies, University of Mumbai. He begins his career as Lecturer of Business Management for MBA in 1992 under university of Pune and remain in that position for four years. He is doctorate in Business Management and M. Phil, in Business Administration. He has 30 Years of experience in the field of Industry. Teaching. Research and leading management and Professional institutions of repute.

His academic contribution and leadership has been applauding by industry and academic fraternity. He received around 26 Awards, Honors & Fellowships for outstanding contributions. Some of them are International Youth Fellowship from world education leader's forum held at Germany in 2015 in presence. He has been awarded for Academic leadership for his contribution to higher education through leading, teaching and research by Higher Education Forum of India (HEF). He has been felicitated by Ministry of Industry. Government of Maharashtra for his contribution made towards Industry 2016. listed in Top 50 national personalities in India Matters (Biographic Compendium of Indian Express 2008) for contribution to Nation and iconic intervention in India's Progress.

He is certified Corporate Directors from World Council of Corporate Governance. (UK) His research areas are Information Technology & Systems, Digital Business. Artificial Intelligence. Business & Technology Strategy etc. His research work is laudable; He is reviewer & Member on editorial board of various international & National journals; his 156 Research Papers has been published in (Web of Science. ADBC, Scopus. UGC Care List, Double Blind Review) with High Impact reputed International & National Journals. Good numbers of Minor and Major Business Research Projects are on his credits. He authored and edited 5 books. Successfully guided 12 Ph. D's and 5 M Phil students and more than 1000 PG projects. He has organised & curated and conducted more than 250 Seminar, Conferences, Workshops, Symposium, FDP/ MDP programmes on diversified areas of management and verticals of industry and also delivered address in more than 100 Conferences, Seminars. He played pivotal role in reforming teaching, learning process and taken various innovative and strategic initiatives to prepare

twenty first century management graduates and implemented various student centric education policies at Jamnalal Bajaj Institute of Management Studies, For Academic

Assignment he has travelled to Germany. France, South Africa, Netherland and Switzerland, Dubai and an across India etc.

He was the Chairman Board of studies in System Management and Academic Council member, University of Mumbai, He is Member of Research and Review Committee (RRC) of three state Universities, Mumbai, Pune and SNDT University. He is Member board of management studies, Mumbai University and Pune University. He was member to draft on line management education policy, Govt, of India, two years he was member on E- Governance initiative and implementation committee for Govt, of Maharashtra.

Two years he was Executive Board member of Association of Indian Management Schools (AIMS). He is Member on various boards like Bombay Stock Exchange, Council of Fair Business Practices of India, Employee Federation of India, Confederation of Indian Industries (CII), Institution of Director, Bombay Management Associations. Assessor of NBA, AICTE, DTE, and various many management and professional institutions and universities etc.

Dr. Sushma Patil is working as an Associate Professor-Operations and Supply Chain Management in Vivekanand Education Society's Vivekanand Business School, Mumbai. Dr. Sushma is Doctorate from Jamnalal Bajaj Institute of Management, Mumbai. She has completed MBA from North Maharashtra University and Graduate in Pharmacy from Pune University. She has rich academic experience of around 14 years in various management colleges across Mumbai. She has presented various research papers in National and International journals and attended national and international conferences, FDPs, workshops and seminars. She is recipient of Best research paper award at various national and international conferences. Dr. Sushma has successfully completed online certification Program on Design Thinking and Innovation from Harward Business School.

Name	:	**Girish Arun Karandikar**
Nationality	:	Indian
Date of Birth	:	May 23, 1965
Marital Status	:	Married
Permanenet Address	:	C/107, Prakash Nagar, New Mogul Lane, Mahim, Mumbai- 400 016,
Contact No.	:	91 22 24377011/ 24225334, 9819325334
Email	:	gkenterprise.65@gmail.com karandikar.girish@yahoo.com
Languages	:	English, Japanese, Hindi, Gujarati and Marathi
Education	:	B.E. (ELECTRICAL) – 1987, 1st class with Distinction, Ranked 6TH in Shivaji University

Certified Lead Auditor for ISO certifications

- School: Balmohan Vidya Mandir-Dadar, Mumbai
- College: D G Ruparel college-Matunga, Mumbai
- Degree College: Walchand College of Engineering Sangli

Major Achievements

- 1ST class with distinction ranked 6TH in Shivaji University for B. E. exam
- Selected for Hitachi, scholarship by AOTS-JAPAN.
- Received appreciation from all the Employers-Tata, L&T, Hitachi and Danway
- Lead Auditor and internal auditor for ISO--9001/14001/22000/27001/ 45001/ 13485/TS 16949
- Worked with world class companies in ISO and Engineering Segment

Training

- M/s. Tata Consulting Engineers-Design & cost Estimates for tenders, Inspection & Testing of Electrical systems Equipments and power stations
- M/s. Hitachi Ltd., JAPAN for Quality Management and Japanese Management system

Gas Insulated Sub-station-GIS, Design & Testing

- M/s Larsen &Toubro—Project Management, Effective communication systems, Problem solving, Leader effectiveness, RTSC (Real time strategic change) management

Experience in India

- M/s. Tata Consulting Engineers
- M/s Larsen &Toubro Ltd.
- M/s G.K. Enterprise from 2000 till date

Experience International

- M/s. Danway, U.A.E.
- M/s Hitachi UAE
- M/s Hitachi Ltd. JAPAN

Engineering and Inspection Activity

- Industrial: GMRT-for TIFR. and Float glass Mirror line facility
- Infrastructure: Development of Industrial Area - Sharjah.
- Building Automation: Tata Research Centre.
- Nuclear Plant: Tarapur Atomic Power project - Unit 3 & 4,500 MW
- GIS -- 220 KV GIS substations for Tata Power, AL-Taweelah (U.A.E.) 400 kV GIS
- Chemical Projects --Propylene Terminal facility-RIL, Ethylene and LPG storage tanks- Finolex Industry, Saudi formaldehyde plant.

Design Work

- Preparation of SLD & Load flow reviews, Specification of Electrical Equipments
- Tender Analysis, Cable schedules and Estimates of bill of material
- Layout Drawings for cabling, lighting, Earth system review and Switchyard systems
- Erection contract specifications, Layouts /GA and review of Schematic diagrams

Installation and Inspection

- Transformer, Motors, Switchgear –HT/LT. Panels, Capacitor. RTU panels, Power plant
- Cables and cable trays, Motor control centers, Fabrication work, Pressure vessel, Project audit, Galvanizing unit, Heat treatment unit, Forging and automobile items etc.

Engineering--EPC Projects

- Power and Distribution transformers, H.V.&L.V. switchgear MCC, Motors Lighting items, Cables and Earthing items.RIL-PTF project, Finolex plant, Industrial plants
- Chemical plants, Thermal power plant, Solar plant and DG Set

Electrical and Fire Safety audits

- Conduct electrical safety audit for industry and for institutes, Fire safety audits for various organizations and training for industrial safety systems.

Software

- ETAP (Electrical transient analyzer program).
- PDS (Plant design system).
- CAD & Office 365

ISO Certifications

- Lead Auditor and worked as certification auditor, Worked as consultant for
- ISO 9001/14001/20000/22000/27001/45001/50001/IATF-16949/ 22301/ CMMI/13485/SA 8000
- Consultancy work covering Process establishment, Procedures as per the requirements of ISO Std. Formats and reporting system.
- Training activity cover -- awareness, implementation and internal auditor training
- Auditing –covering internal and third-party audits.
- Worked on the panel of certification body as certification auditor.

ESG Work

Work involved following activities

- Understand present working using gap audit and Business impact analysis-BIA.
- Establish process flow of overall working of the company.
- Define list of processes and activities within process covering environmental Aspect and impact analysis covering air quality, water quality and PCB norms as per ISO 14001
- Release process flow chart covering all activities and roles. Establish MIS for ESG reporting to Management
- Succession planning to ensure business continuity.
- Identify risk and opportunities for each process considering health, safety, and social accountabilities.
- Define and approve communication systems covering all the process and related activities.
- Ensure legal compliance and establish review system for monitoring as per SA 8000.
- Release of documentation for implementation covering quality ,environment, occupational health, and safety as well as governance based international std .ISO 45001
- Conduct training on implementation and documents as per the Information security guidelines as per ISO 27001
- Guidance for Energy management and fire safety using electrical and fire safety audits.

- Conduct periodic performance improvement audits to eliminate or reduce risk.
- Work as Panel auditor for Lloyds, ISC, ICL, QSS and 10 plus certification bodies
- Conduct Job profitability review audits.

International Clients—

Worked with international brands having offices and factories all over Asia and Europe. Some of the client details are as listed below—

• Voestalpine group
• Apollo Group
• Thyssen group
• Bohler -Uddeholm ind. Pvt. Ltd
• Al Faara Group
• Emirates Logistics
• Kawashima Rubber
• American Tank and Fabricators
• Nestle Health care
• Ascendas-First Space -AFS
• Lupin Healthcare
• BASF
• Exusia
• Baker Tilly

Working Experience for various Countries

Worked in **HITACHI--JAPAN**

Aware of Asian culture and methodology of working as many of Japanese companies' vendors are from Malaysia, Indonesia and Thailand. Have worked with clients from Russia, Singapore ,Dubai and Germany

Training and Courses

- Conducted training for ISO awareness, Internal auditor and Lead Auditor
- Course on World class manufacturing in Chetna college and staff Skill upgradation in ICT
- Japanese Language in SCOFL (Study Centre of Foreign Languages)

Major Customers in INDIA

- Worked for more than 500 customers --L&T, M&M, IL&FS, JNPT, Nestle, Saraswat bank, Future group, Reliance Infra, Grasim-Birla, Essel World, HPCL, Thyssen group, NIIF-National infra investment fund ,Apollo supply chain and MSME Industries
- Customers in Manufacturing, service, and project industry in more than 30 plus segments

Advanced Supply Chain Management and Logistics in Agriculture

Compiled by

Prashant S. Bodake
Dean & Director of Instruction, DBSKKV
Co-ordinator & Principal Investigator
NAHEP-IDP, DBSKKV-Dapoli, Maharashtra

Srinivasan Iyengar
Director of Jamnalal Bajaj Institute of Management Studies
Mumbai, Maharashtra

Rajesh T. Thokal
Co- Principal Investigator, NAHEP-IDP, DBSKKV-Dapoli, Maharashtra

Authors

Chandrahauns Chavan
Senior Professor & Former Director
Jamnalal Bajaj Institute of Management Studies
University of Mumbai, Mumbai, Maharashtra

Sushma Patil
Associate Professor
Vivekanand Business School, Mumbai, Maharashtra

Girish Arun Karandikar
ISO Expert
C/107, Prakash Nagar, New Mogul Lane, Mahim, Mumbai, Maharashtra

Indian Council of Agricultural Research (ICAR)

Dr. Balasaheb Sawant Konkan Krishi Vidyapeeth (DBSKKV)

National Agricultural Higher Education Project-Institutional Development Plan (NAHEP-IDP)

NIPA® Genx Electronic Resources & Solutions P. Ltd., New Delhi-110 034

Citation: National Agriculture Higher Education Project Institutional Development Plan, DBSKKV, Dapoli & ICAR, New Delhi

NIPA® GENX ELECTRONIC RESOURCES & SOLUTIONS P. LTD.

101,103, Vikas Surya Plaza, CU Block
L.S.C.Market, Pitam Pura, New Delhi-110 034
Ph : +91 11 27341616, 27341717, 27341718
E-mail: newindiapublishingagency@gmail.com
Website: www.nipabooks.com

For customer assistance, please contact
Phone: + 91-11-27 34 17 17
Fax: + 91-11-27 34 16 16

ISBN: 978-93-58870-95-4

Composed and Designed by NIPA®.

भारतीय कृषि अनुसंधान परिषद
कृषि अनुसंधान भवन–II, नई दिल्ली–110012
INDIAN COUNCIL OF AGRICULTURAL RESEARCH
KRISHI ANUSANDHAN BHAVAN-II, PUSA, NEW DELHI-110012
Phone: +91-11-25841760
Email: ddg.edu@icar.gov.in, ddgedn@gmail.com, nd.nahep@icar.gov.in

Dr. Rakesh Chandra Agrawal
Deputy Director General (Agril. Edn.)

Message

It is with immense pleasure and a sense of purpose that I provide this forward to the National Agricultural Higher Education Project-Institutional Development Plan (NAHEP-IDP) at Dr. Balasaheb Sawant Konkan Krishi Vidyapeeth (DBSKKV) and the concurrent endeavour to develop a short pilot course in skilling small-scale agri-entrepreneurship. This transformative initiative is under the guidance and leadership of the Hon'ble Vice Chancellor of DBSKKV Dr.S.G.Bhave.

Principal Investigator of NAHEP-IDP, DBSKKV-Dapoli Dr. P.S.Bodake, a distinguished and visionary leader in the field of agriculture, has consistently championed the cause of advancing agricultural education, research, and extension services. His strategic vision has played a pivotal role in shaping the trajectory of agricultural development in our nation, with a keen focus on empowering farming communities and fostering innovation.

The NAHEP-IDP of DBSKKV stands as a testament to ICAR & World Bank commitment to elevating the standards of agricultural education. By providing institutional support and promoting excellence across various facets of academia, research, and extension activities, the project aims to position DBSKKV as a center of excellence in agricultural learning and research.

In tandem with the NAHEP-IDP, the initiation of a short pilot course in skilling smallscale agri-entrepreneurship reflects DBSKKV foresight in addressing contemporary challenges in agriculture. Recognizing the pivotal role played by small-scale agri-entrepreneurs in driving rural economies, this course is designed to equip them with the necessary skills and knowledge to navigate the dynamic landscape of agribusiness.

The NAHEP-IDP, DBSKKV envisions this pilot course as a stepping stone toward fostering a culture of entrepreneurship in agriculture. By blending theoretical insights with practical applications, the course seeks to empower agri-entrepreneurs, enabling them to adopt sustainable farming practices, embrace innovation, and contribute significantly to the economic prosperity of their communities.

I extend my heartfelt appreciation to Dr. P.S. Bodake and his entire NAHEP-IDP Team for their steadfast leadership and unwavering commitment to advancing agricultural education and entrepreneurship. Under his guidance, these initiatives are poised to make a lasting impact on the agricultural education landscape and the entrepreneurial spirit within the students and farming community.

(R.C. Agrawal)
Deputy Director General (Agril. Edn.)

DR. BALASAHEB SAWANT KONKAN KRISHI VIDYAPEETH
Dapoli, Dist. Ratnagiri - 415712
Tel. No.: (0)02358-282064, **Fax No.**: 02358-282074, **Mob.**: 9422556565
E-mail : vcdbskkv-mh@gov.in, ipmbhave@gmail.com, **website** : www.dbskkv.org

Dr. Sanjay G. Bhave
IDP Leader
Vice Chancellor, DBSKKV

Message

I am delighted to present the Institutional Development Plan as part of the National Agricultural Higher Education Project (NAHEP) undertaken by our esteemed institution. This initiative marks a significant milestone in our commitment to advancing agricultural education, research, and innovation, with the ultimate goal of transforming the agricultural landscape of our nation.

This pilot course serves as a testament to our university's dedication to fostering innovation and fostering collaboration between academia and industry. We believe that by offering this course, we are not only contributing to the skill development of individuals but also playing a pivotal role in shaping the future of agriculture.

We at DBSKKV are happy to felicitate the proficient attainment of the Principal Investigator, IDP Coordinator, and Dean and Director of Instruction of DBSKKV-Dr.Prashant S. Bodake and team NAHEP-IDP involved in the same vertical. Your magnificent work makes all of us highly gratified and prosperous. Well Done!

I extend my gratitude to the faculty members, industry experts, and stakeholders who have contributed their expertise and insights to the development of this course. Their collective efforts have ensured that the curriculum aligns with the ever-changing demands of the agricultural sector.

I am excited to witness the impact that this short pilot course on skilling small-scale agricultural entrepreneurship will have on our participants and, consequently, on the agricultural landscape. With this initiative, we are sowing the seeds of empowerment and innovation, cultivating a new generation of agripreneurs who will not only navigate challenges but also unearth opportunities for growth.

(Sanjay G. Bhave)
IDP Leader
Vice Chancellor, DBSKKV

NATIONAL AGRICULTURAL HIGHER EDUCATION PROJECT
AGRICULTURAL EDUCATION DIVISION
INDIAN COUNCIL OF AGRICULTURAL RESEARCH
(Department of Agricultural Research and Education
Ministry of Agriculture and Farmers Welfare, Government of India)
Room No. 514, Krishi Anusandhan Bhawan-II, Pusa, New Delhi-110 012

Date : 14.12.2023

Dr. N.K. Jain
National Coordinator (IDP)

Message

It is a matter of great pleasure to learn that Dr. Balasaheb Sawant Konkan Krishi Vidyapeeth, Dapoli has developed short pilot course on "Skilling Small-scale Agri-Entrepreneurship" for the undergraduate students. The efforts made by DBSKKV, Dapoli and the Knowledge Experts is a significant stride towards fostering interdisciplinary learning and preparing students for the evolving landscape of agriculture. Agriculture, the backbone of our nation, is undergoing a transformative phase that demands a comprehensive understanding of not only traditional farming practices but also entrepreneurial skills. In this context, DBSKKV, Dapoli is driven by the vision to equip undergraduate students with the knowledge and skills necessary to navigate the complexities of modern agriculture and contribute to the burgeoning field of agri-entrepreneurship. I commend the leadership of Dr. S.G. Bhave, Hon'ble Vice Chancellor, DBSKVV, Dapoli for his forward-thinking approach in embracing this initiative and commitment to provide a robust academic environment aligns seamlessly with our objective of preparing students for the dynamic and competitive landscape of agriculture and entrepreneurship.

I also congratulate Dr. P.S. Bodake, Principal Investigator of NAHEP-IDP, DBSKKV, Dapoli and his entire team, whose collaborative efforts have been instrumental in shaping the curriculum of this course. Together, we envision a program that not only imparts knowledge but also nurtures a spirit of inquiry and enterprise among the students. I extend my warmest congratulations to the University on the launch of the innovative short pilot course on "Skilling Small-scale Agri-Entrepreneurship". May this endeavour be a beacon of progress, fostering excellence in agricultural education and empowering the next generation of agri-entrepreneurs. University's commitment to bridging theory and practical is commendable, and I am confident that this initiative will contribute significantly to the growth of our agricultural landscape.

Place: New Delhi

(N. K. Jain)

Mob. No.: 9420413255 / 8275201130
Email.: (P)prameghash@gmail.com (O) hodagrodapoli@gmail.com (O) piidpdbskkv@gmail.com (O)nodalcelldbskkv@gmail.com

Dr. P. S. Bodake
Dean & Director of Instruction
Coordinator, Principal Investigator, NAHEP-IDP

Message

It is with immense pride and anticipation that I present the Institutional Development Plan as part of our active involvement in the National Agricultural Higher Education Project (NAHEP). This plan embodies our institution's unwavering commitment to redefining agricultural education and research, and it signifies a transformative journey towards excellence and innovation.

Through this plan, we aim to enhance our institutional capacities, bolster research initiatives, and cultivate strategic partnerships with industries and communities. By incorporating modern pedagogical techniques, fostering interdisciplinary collaboration, and harnessing the potential of emerging technologies, we strive to create a learning ecosystem that empowers our students to become leaders and change-makers in the agricultural sector and it will not only elevate our institution's stature but also propel the agricultural education and research landscape towards a brighter and more sustainable future.

Our joint commitment to education and empowerment has culminated in the creation of this pilot course. Through a harmonious blend of theoretical insights and practical experiences, participants will delve into market trends, value chain analysis, sustainable practices, financial management, and the integration of technology into agriculture. This holistic approach is designed to prepare individuals to navigate the intricacies of agripreneurship with confidence.

This pilot course is an embodiment of our dedication to fostering collaboration between academia and industry. By bridging the gap between theory and practice, we aim to nurture a new generation of agripreneurs who are poised to steer the agricultural sector towards innovation and growth.

We sincerely mention primitive gratitude towards the former Vice-chancellor of DBSKKV Dr. Sanjay D. Sawant and Vice-chancellor of DBSKKV Dr. Sanjay G. Bhave for such prudent leadership and providence. We feel proud to highlight the sheer hard work and great dedication of the Co-Principal Investigator of NAHEP-IDP and IDP Staff.

We are grateful to the Director of Jamnalal Bajaj Institute of Management-Mumbai Dr. Shrinivasan Iyengar for such excellent association and cordial congruence in the course of developing a short pilot course in skilling small-scale Agri-Entrepreneurship. We also express our sincere gratitude to the faculty members of JBIMS & University of Mumbai, industry experts, and stakeholders whose expertise and contributions have shaped this course. Their collective wisdom ensures that the curriculum remains attuned to the evolving demands of the agricultural landscape.

Thank you.

(P. S. Bodake)
Dean & Director of Instruction
Coordinator, Principal Investigator, NAHEP-IDP

Preface

This book specially aims to provide students with a fundamental understanding of basic and advanced concepts of supply chain management and logistics. It highlights the role of supply chain and logistics particularly in agricultural sector.

The book has its own unique features. It brings out the subject in a very simple and lucid manner for easy and comprehensive understanding of the basic concepts, its intricacies, procedures and practices. This book will help the readers to have a broader view on Supply Chain and Logistics Management. The language used in this book is easy and understandable. It will help students to improve their vocabulary of Logistics terms and understand the matter in a better and happier way.

The book is divided into six chapters.

The first chapter focusses on detailed explanation on basic concepts of supply chain and logistics with definitions, scope of Logistics and SCM, and its significance.

The second chapter emphasizes the basic concepts agricultural supply chain and its role in overall development of economy. It also focusses on various issues and challenges faced by Indian agricultural supply chain.

The third chapter introduces the concept of ARID (Agricultural and rural income diversification). It covers concepts like diversification, determinants of diversification etc.

The book not only explains the basic aspects but also views supply chain from a broad and global perspective. In relation to that Chapter four majorly focuses on deep insights of concepts of digital supply chain management and its impact on supply chain efficiency and responsiveness. It gives insights about various technologies used in supply chain management.

Chapter five emphasizes on the role of packaging in agricultural supply chain. It mainly covers its importance, types of various packaging material available in market along with its merits and demerits.

With growing importance of quality aspects and its significance in supply chain, this book in chapter six explains role of ISO in supply chain management.

Authors

Contents

1

Introduction of Supply Chain Management

1.1 Supply Chain Management (SCM)

Mentzer *et al.* (2001) defined SCM as 'the systematic, strategic coordination of the traditional business functions within a particular organization and across businesses within the supply chain, for the purposes of improving the long-term performance of the individual companies and the supply chain as a whole'. According to Walters and Lancaster (2000), supply chain management is the management of the interface relationships among key stakeholders and business functions that occur in the maximization of value creation which is driven by customer needs satisfaction and facilitated by efficient logistics management.

The supply chain encompasses every effort involved in producing and delivering a final product from the supplier's supplier to the customer's customer (Supply Chain Council,2002) The primary goal of SCM is effectively managing the flow of materials and information from supply sources to the final point of sale. SCM has also been described as the management of raw materials, in process materials and finished-goods inventories from the point of origin to the point of consumption and the planning and control of materials and information from suppliers to end customers (Zsidisin *et al.,* 2000).

Elmuti (2002) defined supply chain management as the works to bring the supplier, the distributor and the customer into one cohesive process. Thus, traditional aspect of SCM for involving only two parties that is buyers and suppliers is extended to technology enabled supply chain and involvement of all members. Each supply chain member is responsible for specific added value function in relation to the product/service as it progresses towards the final consumer. According to Mowat & Collins (2000), understanding and meeting consumer needs has principal importance in SCM as a way of optimizing value to customers and improving return to all stakeholders in the supply chain. It shows that SCM has the responsibility to follow customer-driven culture.

Supply chain management (SCM) often refers to the process oriented management approach to sourcing, producing, delivering goods and services to end customers and to the coordination of various actors belonging to the same supply chain as cooperation in SCM paves way to competitive advantage (Christopher and Juttner, 2000).

SCM addresses the integration of organizational functions ranging from the ordering and receipt of raw materials through the manufacturing processes to the distribution and delivery of products to customers with a view to enable organizations to achieve higher quality in products and customer service in order to lower inventory costs for enhancing competitive advantage (Ohdar and Pradip, 2006; Stevens, 1989).

Supply chain management (SCM) is a central and important area for academic research due to its impact on firms competing in today's global economy, and supply chain management is recognized as a contemporary concept that leads in achieving benefits of both operational and strategic nature (Al-Mudimigh, Zairi, and Ahmed, 2004).

According to Gunasekaran, Patel and McGaughey (2004), at the strategic level, SCM is a relatively new and rapidly expanding discipline that is transforming the way for improving organizational competitiveness both in manufacturing and services.

Christopher (1998) defines SCM as the management of upstream and downstream relationships with suppliers and customers to deliver superior customer value at less cost to the Supply chain as a whole.

SCM as the process of strategically managing the movement and storage of materials, parts and finished inventory from suppliers through the firm to customers. SCM is the effort involved in producing and delivering a final product from a supplier's supplier to the customer's customer (Johnston ,1995).

SCM as a co-ordinated approach for managing the flow of goods from suppliers to ultimate customers, and that the goal is to meet customer service objectives while minimising inventory and related cost Carter *et al.* (1995). Simchi-Levy (2000) states that "Supply Chain Management is a set of approaches utilized to efficiently integrate suppliers, manufactures, warehouses and stores, so that merchandise is produced and distributed at the right quantities, to the right locations, and at the right time, in order to minimize system wide costs while satisfying service level requirements"

Thus, traditional objective of SCM is to minimize the total supply chain cost to meet fixed and given demand such as raw material and other acquisition costs, inbound transportation cost, facility investment costs, outbound transportation cost but advanced SCM objective is along with cost efficiency, to bring responsiveness also by focussing needs of the customer with respect to time and availability of goods and services. For that SCM involves all chain members, right from the supplier, supplier's supplier and to the end consumer.

1.2 Different Structures of Supply Chain

According to Annelie Pettersson (2008), the Supply chain structure differs between different types of products and services. Examples of three types of general Supply chains are:

1. Supply chain for products that are sold in a store outlet
2. Supply chain for products that are ordered from a supplier by customer
3. Supply chain for services.

Fig. 1.1.1: Supply chain for products sold in a store

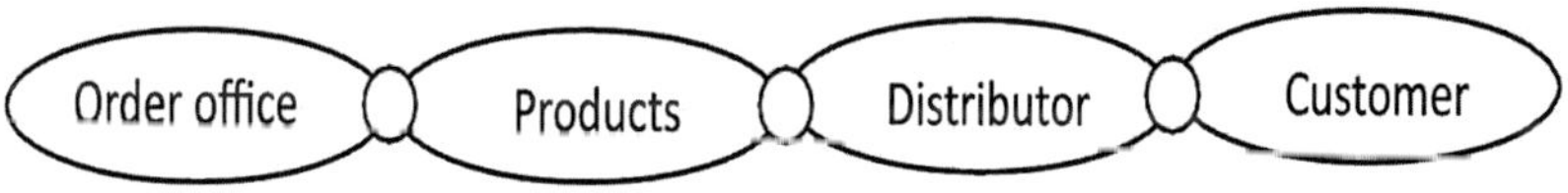

Fig. 1.1.2: Supply chain for products ordered from a supplier

Fig. 1.2.3: Supply chain for a service

In the grocery industry, customers go directly to a store and purchase what they would like to have. The Supply chain in figure 3.1 starts with the customer placing an order to the supplier. The supplier books the order and starts production. The product is then delivered to the customer. Specific for Supply chains for services on the other hand, is that no physical product is delivered. The service can be delivered in many different ways, such as in a hair salon, by mail or by phone. Irrespective of the differences between what function of the company that is taking part of the Supply chain and how the product or service is delivered, the term Supply chain is applicable to describe the chain.

One common thing for all Supply chains is that all actors in the flow are suppliers to the end customer. Fisher (1997) said that the reason for problems in many Supply chains has been a mismatch between the product type and the type of Supply chain. A customer can require different Supply chains over time. It is important for a supplier to have the right Supply chain for a customer in different business situations. Decision of the right supply chain is based on the type of product/service.

Hoover *et al.* (2001) innovated a concept describing customer relationship is needed to take the next step in modification of SCM. This step is to create Demand-Supply chains. The purpose of the Demand chain thinking is to give the customer an extended choice that also includes the relationship level. Demand-Supply Chain Management requires a closer co-operation between the Supply function and the Marketing & Sales function in a company.

Outsourcing is also major part of the supply chain. One of the most important trends in the second half of 1990 has been the concentration to core business and it generated the concept of outsourcing. More outsourcing means that the Supply chain is increasing and it gets more important to manage the Supply chain. It is important to be part of the right chain according to Paulsson *et al.* (2003).

1.3 The Scope of Supply Chain Management

SCM has a wide scope. Many companies are discovering that efficient Supply Chain Management is what they need to focus on in order to increase profit and market share. There are companies that have reduced their manufacturing cost as much as is practically possible. The company has to focus on the whole Supply chain to find new areas where cost can be reduced. Many firms have moved aggressively to improve SCM to balance customers demand with the need for profitable growth. Hoover *et al.* (2001) mean that a difficult part of SCM is to offer better value to the customer and at the same time reduce costs. Hoover *et al.* (2001) state that the objective of SCM is efficiency improvements of the product delivery process from raw material suppliers to the end customer in accordance with. The primary purpose for the efficient Supply chain is to fulfil demand at the lowest possible cost. The objective of SCM is efficiency improvements of the product delivery process from raw material suppliers to the end customer. SCM can also impact the important customer value of price by significantly reducing costs. Customer value is also important for determining the type of Supply chain required to retain customers. A customer driven Supply chain strategy is determined by the type of products or services it offers and the value of various elements of this offering to the customer.

Simchi-Levy (2000) mentioned that Supply Chain Management takes into consideration every facility that has an impact on cost and plays a role in making the product reaches to customer requirements. The objective of Supply Chain Management is to be efficient and cost effective across the entire system.

Cost efficiency means consideration of the total system wide costs, from transportation and distribution to inventories of raw materials, work in process and finished goods and that the cost is minimized. Supply Chain Management is not simply about minimizing transportation cost and reducing inventories, but to increase responsiveness also.

Decisions in Supply Chain Management

SCM involves different types of decisions like strategic, tactical and operational decisions. The strategic level deals with decision that have long–lasting effect on the firm. This includes decisions regarding the number, location and capacity of warehouses and flow of material through the logistics network. The tactical level includes decisions that are typically updated anywhere between once every quarter and once every year. These include sourcing and procurement decisions, inventory strategies and transportation policies including the frequency with which customers are visited. The operational level refers to day-to-day decisions such as scheduling, lead- time quotations, routing and truck loading. All these activities have to be considered when setting up a Supply chain SCM spans over all levels in a company.

Annelie Pettersson (2008) also said that SCM includes activities from purchasing, order handling, production and distribution. All these activities have to be considered when setting up a Supply chain. Following shows activities in SCM.

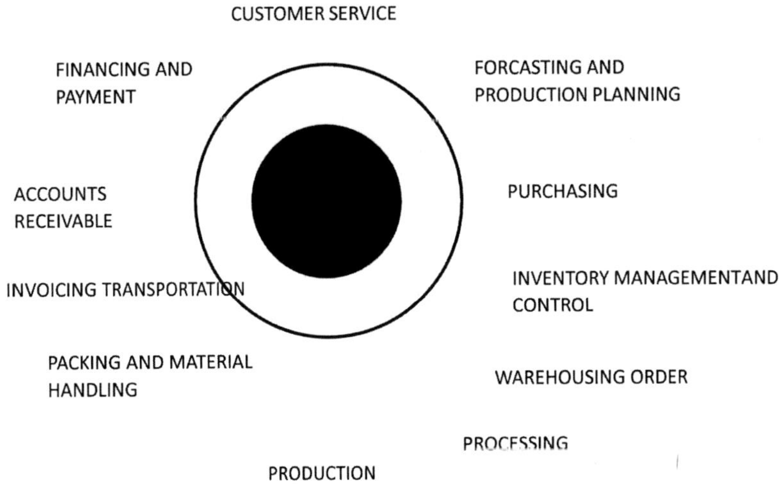

Activities within a company in SCM.

1.4 Different types of flows in supply chain

Any type of supply chain (for manufacturing or service industry) involves three types of flows that are product flow, information flow and monetary flow.

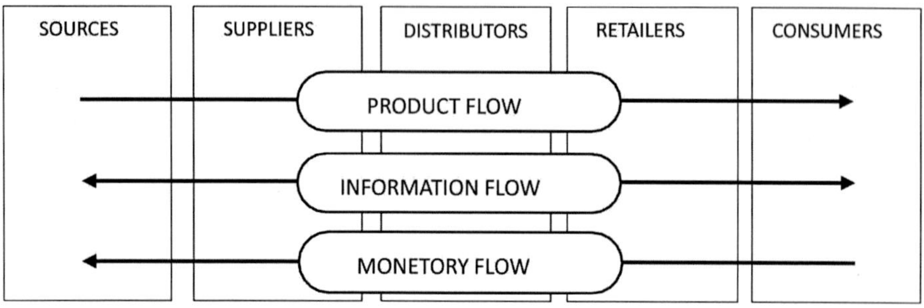

Three flows in SCM There are multiple flows that need to be managed in industrial companies. Two of the most important ones in supply chain management are material flows and information flows. Material flows refer to products being transported between and within different supply chain nodes. Information flows refer to transferring information between the supply chain nodes, both upstream and downstream, on aspects such as customer orders, demand forecasts, inventory levels and capacity availability. Such information can be shared with some nodes and not with others, and can be updated with varying frequencies. Besides material and information flows, there are also money, manpower and capital equipment flow. It is critical to understand that all of these flows are not independent from each other but are interlinked and influence each other in ways that are difficult to predict.

2

Agricultural Supply Chain

An agriculture supply chain system comprises organizations/cooperatives that are responsible for the production and distribution of vegetable/Fruits/Cereals/Pulses or animal-based products. In general, we distinguish two main types:

1. 'Agriculture food supply chains for fresh agricultural products' (such as fresh vegetables, flowers, fruit). In general, these chains may comprise growers, auctions, wholesalers, importers and exporters, retailers and speciality shops and their input and service suppliers. Basically, all of these stages leave the intrinsic characteristics of the product grown or produced untouched. The main processes are the handling, conditioned storing, packing, transportation and especially trading of these goods.
2. 'Agriculture food supply chains for processed food products' (such as portioned meats, snacks, juices, desserts, canned food products). In these chains, agricultural products are used as raw materials for producing consumer products with higher added value. In most cases, conservation and conditioning processes extend the shelf-life of the products.

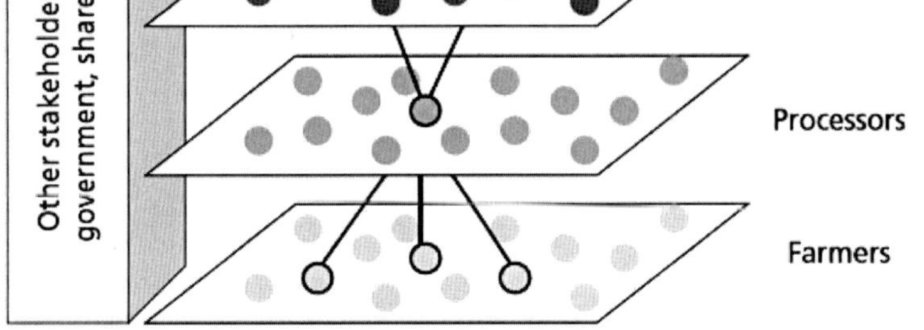

2.1 Issues Related to Agriculture Supply Chains

1. Participants in Agriculture supply chains, e.g. farmers, traders, processors, retailers, etc, understand that original good quality products can be subject to quality decay because of an inadequate action of another participant.
2. For example, when a farm leaves a can of milk for pick-up on a roadside, under the sun, without any cover, there will be a loss of quality that may even render the raw material unfit for processing.
3. Similarly, if processors, on the other hand, use packaging items and/or technologies that do not maintain freshness and nutritional characteristics of their products as much as possible, retailers will be likely to face customer complaints.

2.2 Characteristics of Agriculture Supply Chains and its Impact on Logistics

Supply Chain Stage	**Issues with Product & Process Characteristics**	**Impact on Logistic/Flowof goods.**
Overall	Shelf-life constraints for raw materials, intermediates and finished products and changesin product quality level while progressing the supply chain (decay). Recycling of Materials Required.	• Timing constraints (goods have to be supplied quickly to avoiddecay). • Information requirements (correct information of goods is essential).
Growers / Producers	• Long production times (producing new or additionalagro-products takes a lot of time) • Seasonality in production • Variability of quality and quantity of supply	• Responsiveness • Flexibility in process and planning
Auctions / Wholesalers/ Retailers	• Variability of quality and quantity of supply of farm-based inputs • Seasonal supply of productsrequires global (year-round)sourcing • Requirements for conditioned transportation and storage means	• Pricing issues • Timing constraints • Need for conditioning • Pre-information on quality status of products

2.3 Agriculture value chain

The agriculture value chain concept has been used since the beginning of the millennium, although there is no universally accepted definition for the term. It normally refers to the whole range of goods and services necessary for an agricultural product to move from farm to its final customer. The World Bank's definition of the term "value chain" describes the full range of value adding activities required to bring a product or service through the different phases of production, including procurement of raw materials and other inputs".

Recent trends are prompting an increasingly urgent question around the sustainability of value creation in the future. The extreme weather volatility, growing food demand, and wide gap in the agriculture productivity between India and its peers in the region, and the need to manage food prices and import pulses to meet demand have all highlighted that India needs to rethink its approach.

In a significant mindset shift, the government's focus is moving from increasing farm output to improving farmer incomes. It has set an aspiration to double farmers' incomes by 2022 through the follow six key agendas,

- Improvement in crop productivity.
- Improvement in livestock productivity.
- Resource use efficiency or saving in cost of production.
- Increase in cropping intensity.
- Diversification towards high value crops.
- Improvement in real prices received by farmers

This will enhance productivity and have multiplied effects on the larger ecosystem.

2.4 Challenges in the value chain

Indian farmers face multiple challenges, primary among these are excessive stress on land, water and soil health, lack of knowledge/information about high value/growth products, limited exposure to high productivity practices, weak market linkages, inefficient supply chains with high levels of food wastage, and an acute dependence on rainfall. To create an income revolution in the agricultural sector we need to capture the entire value chain right from research to the stage where farmers are able to realise money in their pockets.

Some the key challenges in the upstream of agriculture value chain are:

1. ***Scarcity of resources*** — India's farm resources like land, water, and soil health are hugely stressed. More than half the country faces water stress with withdrawals at 40 to 80 percent of available supply. The labour supply is stressed too; India's labour market is making a natural structural transition from farm to non-farm jobs — agricultural jobs declined by 25 million between 2011 and 2015, while non-farm jobs rose by 33 million. The rising wages for farm labor make it imperative to improve farm productivity through mechanisation and other measures.

2. ***Scope to improve yield*** — Indian crop yields are still significantly lower than other country averages. For example, the average rice yield in India is 3.6 ton/hectare compared to 6.7 ton/hectare in China, similarly Potato yield per hectare is 50% lower than that of US. This could improve by at least 40 to 70 percent with suitable interventions. If productivity does not improve, the country could fail to meet the projected food demand for 2025 and remain dependent on imports of rice, pulses, and Fruits & Vegetables (F&V). To meet the growing demand for pulses, India will need to import around 13 million to 17 million metric tons of pulses by 2025. India would then constitute a very large percentage of global trade volumes in pulses.

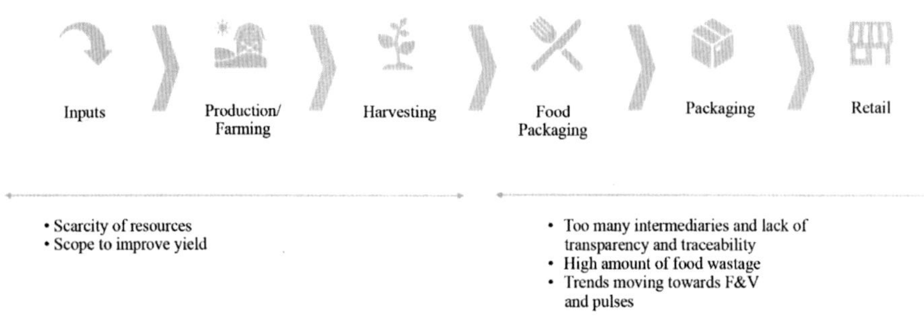

Fig. 2.4.1: Overview of challenges across the value chain

Some the key challenges in the downstream of agriculture value chain are:

1. ***Multiple intermediaries and lack of transparency and traceability*** — Mandis and FPOs need digitisation to bring more transparency into transactions. Farmers need more sales channels. Data and market connect can empower each stakeholder. India ranks among the top 5 countries in food processing. By 2024, the sector will employ 9 mn and the organised sector has only 60% of the share. Streamlining and traceability can improve farmer income and exports

2. ***Losses in the food chain*** — Around 60 percent of food loss and waste in India happens between the field and the end-consumer, and this is concentrated in a few crops especially F&V and cereals. Several challenges limit cold chain penetration and adoption — high cost of stable power supply, low capacity utilisation, and limited financing options. These challenges offer a significant opportunity to improve farmer incomes by addressing the storage and handling of food as well as creating market linkages to customers.

3. ***Trends in consumption moving towards F&V and pulses*** — Over time the Indian diet has seen significant shift towards higher protein intake. Increase in GDP per capita, changes customer preferences towards healthy foods, leading to increased consumption of proteins especially pulses. Overall the future demand will be driven by F&V and pulses, while wheat will only grow at population growth.This leads to an upstream impact on the type of crops the farmers are focusing on producing.

Given the complexity of Indian agriculture no single policy change or technology shift will move the country towards its dual goals of raising income for smallholder farmers and continuing to strengthen the competitiveness of Indian agriculture.

2.5 Digital opportunities across the agricultural value chain

A large number of digital technologies have to be scaled up, some of which have been done already. For example, India has now rolled out one of the most efficient soil health management systems of any country. The sector is now looking forward to using a large number of digital technologies at the pre-production stage, in production and in the post production.

Some of the key opportunities that can create value and boost farmer income are:

1. ***Digital and analytics*** — Digitisation and analytics will play a critical role in building India's farms of the future. Potential disruptions that could unlock value through the food chain are:

    a. Precision farming including integrating field data, weather patterns to drive agronomic advice to farmers, and yield forecasting

    b. Efficient farm lending with electronic applications, disbursal of loans, insurance payouts linked to weather, field data, Direct Benefits Transfer in agriculture

c. Centralised platform integrating farmers and wholesale markets, to provide timely information for price realisation

d. IoT-based advanced analytics in manufacturing plants to improve availability, throughput, and save costs

2. ***Financing and crop insurance*** — can help in strengthening the ecosystem

   a. *Provide innovative equipment*— financing models to farmers through partnerships with manufacturers, weather forecast agencies, and digital partners.

   b. Offer easy financing for FPOs for community infrastructure for storage and transportation.

   c. Create digital ecosystems for financing and crop insurance.

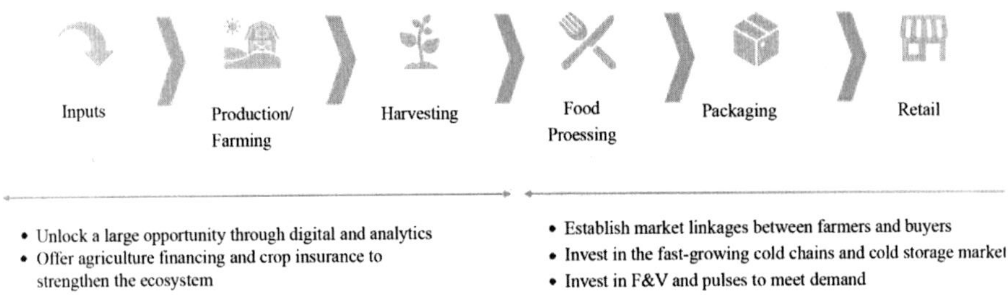

Fig. 2.5.1 : Opportunities in the agriculture value chain

3. ***Establishing market linkages between farmers and buyers*** — This will establish transparency in pricing and better value, especially for perishable products. It could also help to increase farmer incomes by at least 8 to 10 percent. In addition, it will enable the downstream players to source more effectively by eliminating intermediaries. Farmer–producer organisations (FPOs) are already aggregating supply and supporting farmers towards this goal.

4. ***Investing in cold-storage*** — Despite current challenges, this segment is expected to enjoy significant growth on the back of rising food demand, supply deficits, and improved market economics. The cold chain market is expected to double in size to reach $7 billion to $9 billion by end of 2020. Cold chain players could invest in alternate energy technologies like solar-powered systems, they can explore chemical treatments to extend the shelf-life of produce, set up pack houses, and reefer transport. They could also optimize the use of existing facilities by opening them up for multiple crops instead of a single crop or product.

5. ***Invest in F&V and pulses in to meet demand***: These investments could unlock around $15 billion to $20 billion by 2025 and boost farmer income by 35 percent. The value chain of will grow disruptively, with demand concentrated in six crops — mango, tomato, potato, pomegranate, onion, and grapes. By 2025, these six crops will account for around 65 percent of the incremental produce value, through a combination of exports and food processing. In pulses, the demand will be driven by a need for packaged and branded pulses, fortified pulses, and the market for ready-to-eat snacks, which is growing at 20 percent CAGR

2.6 The digital ecosystem in agriculture

The agritech stakeholder ecosystem is rapidly maturing. There are ~450 agritech start-ups in India and growing at 25% year on year. Every 9th agritech start-up in the world is from India. The is huge opportunity to target all the sections of the agriculture value chain.

1. ***Better access to inputs***: Providing better access to agricultural inputs at their doorsteps, it helps farmers to understand the best input to increase yield and productivity
2. ***Financing:*** Farmer struggle to get finance, but agritech based start-ups helps such underserved community of farmers to get loans quickly
3. ***Digital Agriculture***: Digital/ precision agriculture based business offer innovative technology solution to increase farm productivity and farming process efficiency
4. ***Improving the Supply chain***: Market linkage provides a digital platform which connects farm output with customers.
5. ***Farming as a service***: Offers affordable technology solutions for farmers by providing easy access to expensive equipment, converting the fixed costs to variable costs.

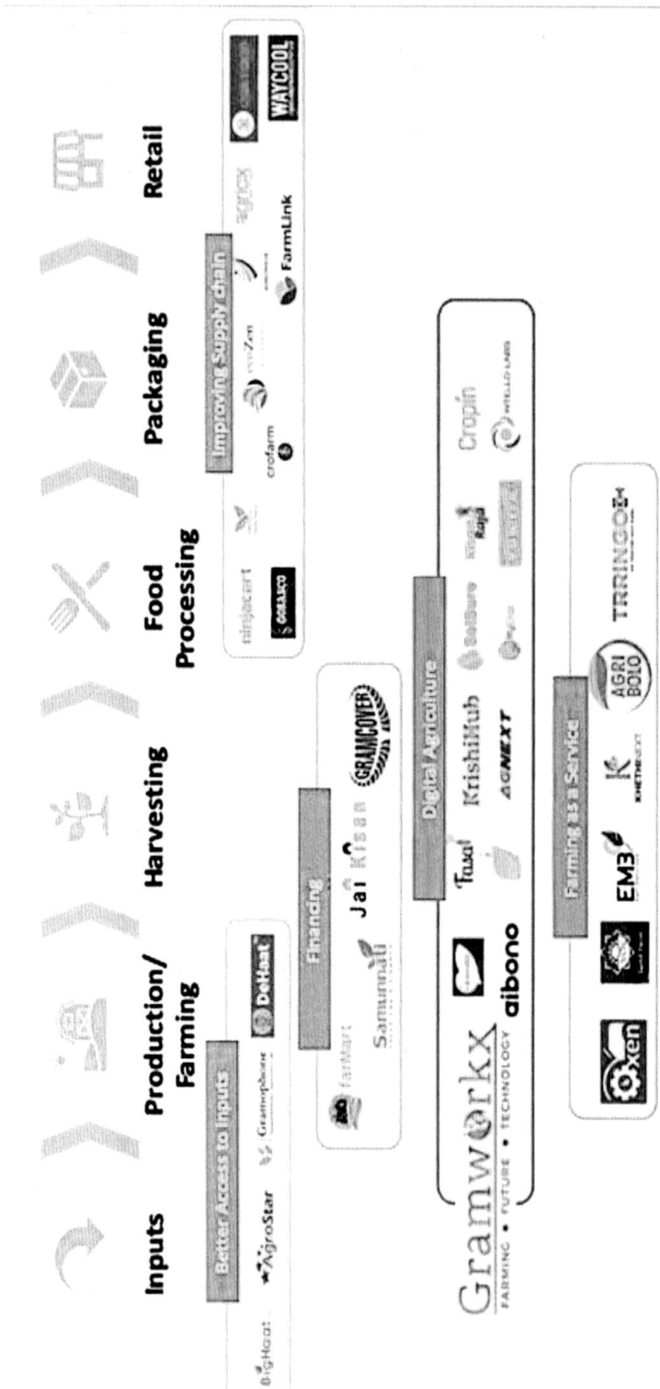

Fig. 2.6.1: Illustrative of the various start-ups in Agritech

3

Agricultural and Rural Income Diversification (ARID)

Agricultural policies in the past have witnessed a series of iterative changes following the economic reforms during the 1990s that marked a Division of Agricultural Economics. Though many of the reform processes were not initiated to directly affect the agriculture sector, it was affected indirectly (Chand, 2004). The mounting stock of food grains has partly been due to the weak purchasing power of the poor in the country. Nevertheless, the problem associated with buffer stock management and degradation of natural resources in some regions has triggered a debate to redefine the agricultural policies. As a remedial measure, it has been suggested that India should diversify its agriculture and get a foothold in the world market (Radhakrishna and Reddy, 2004).

3.1 Diversification

The diversified and accelerated agricultural growth would enhance the food security by improving the purchasing power of the poor in the perplexing situation of shrinkage in agricultural holdings, declining new investments in agriculture and increasing degradation of natural resources (Joshi et al., 2004). Diversification is an integral part of the process of structural transformation of an economy. As in other developing countries, Indian economy is also diversifying at the macro level with the secondary and tertiary sectors becoming progressively more important in terms of their contributions to national income as well as disposition of the workforce. Within the agriculture, some of the sub-sectors are progressively occupying a more significant place than the crop production, and within the crop-mix, the so-called superior cereals are progressing faster than the inferior cereals. However, the factors promoting diversification and the speed with which the changes occur vary under different situations (Vyas, 1996). Moreover, before a sincere attempt is made to suggest policies with regard to diversification, a thorough probe into the pattern and mode of diversification needs to be attempted.. Diversification and Its Components Diversification is basically understood as signifying

3.2 Advance Supply Chain Management & Logistics

the shift from the agricultural to the industrial domain. But, the intricacies underlying the diversification are many and need threadbare understanding. Though the former type of diversification indicates shift from one crop to another crop or from one enterprise/sub-sector to another enterprise/sub-sector, the other type of diversification may involve income-enhancing enterprises in addition to the existing ones. In essence, the diversification to commercial crops/ commodities becomes an essential strategy that can increase incomes in agriculture, minimize risks due to crop failures and above all, earn foreign Singh et al.:

Diversification of Indian Agriculture

Planned diversification increases both individual and social gains (Haque, 1996). This diversification strategy can be designed to help alleviate poverty, generate employment and conserve environment (Hayami and Otsuka, 1995). In India, diversification has occurred both across and within the crop, livestock, forestry and fishery sectors. Within the agriculture, the share of output and employment in the non-crop sectors, i.e. animal husbandry, forestry and fisheries, has been gradually increasing. Thus, diversification is taking place in terms of moving away from crop production to other agricultural activities. More significant changes are taking place within the crop sector, as is evident from the changes in cropping pattern, shown later.

3.3 Determinants of Diversification

Diversification offers a wider choice in the production of crops in the given area. The shift in cultivation from traditional, less-remunerative crops to higher-value crops leads to higher incomes for the producer. At the same time, cultivation of a variety of crops reduces risk. Several factors can induce a shift in the crops grown. These include government policies that promote specific crops, development of infrastructure like roads and markets, and relative profitability of crops.

The major concern of Indian agriculture has been on increasing production of cereals, especially wheat and rice. After achieving self sufficiency in foodgrains and maintaining adequate buffer stocks to meet the generic exigencies, new challenges have given rise to new thrust areas. The present thrust on the ecological and economic access to food through poverty alleviation, higher profits to farmers, sustainability of resources, import substitution, quality improvement and production for exports has led the planners to devise and implement the diversification strategies successfully.

Indian agriculture has witnessed diversification with impressive improvements in the share of livestock and fisheries sector in the total income from agriculture. Within the crop sector, the diversification has largely been in favour of non-foodgrain crops in most of the states. However, the diversification in these states has not been essentially for income generation, but has also been for mitigating risk. The success of any diversification programme involves the development of crop- or enterprise-specific technologies, identification and development of market, and provision of economic incentives. The free trade in the offing envisages the movement from closed to market economies and leaves it to the market, domestic or international, to judge the competitive advantage of a specific product. The competitive advantage and export potential of a country or region for a specific product will depend on the extent to which the crop/commodities grown in the region (a) are competitive in terms of productivity and cost, (b) are remunerative to the farmers, (c) possess export potential and competitiveness in terms of prices, and (d) are able to maintain the quality desired in the international market. India enjoys a comparative advantage due to its diverse agro-eco regions in meeting the challenge posed in the liberalized regime through diversification Singh et al.: Diversification of Indian Agriculture 33 options. However, harnessing the potential of diversification pre-supposes gradual restructuring of diversification-hindering market institutions, infrastructure and quality standards, and credit and fiscal setup into the diversification-encouraging ones. But, certain cautions regarding long-term food security, likely fluctuations in the international market and the element of risk in transitioning from traditional to commercialized agriculture in the presence of sizeable small and marginal farmers must also be kept in mind while speeding up the pace of diversification. The policies are in flux as the economic and political implications of globalization begin to be understood better. There is, however, a consensus that challenges ahead are indeed daunting, requiring greater attention and efforts.

4

Digital Supply Chain Management

Supply Chain is defined as the movement of materials as they flow from their source to the end customer. SCM is a continuously evolving management philosophy that seeks to unify the collective productive competencies and resources of the business functions found both within the enterprise and outside in the firm's allied business partners located along intersecting supply channels into a highly competitive, customer-enriching supply system focused on developing innovative solutions and synchronizing the flow of marketplace products, services, and information to create unique, individualized sources of customer value.

4.1 SCM subsystems

SCM subsystems are important because this is required to support manufacturing managers in making their decisions so that they can optimize the trade off between capital tied up in stocks and inventories, versus the ability to deliver goods at prices and delivery dates agreed with customers.

Typically a SCM consists of these sub-systems can be categorize and consist of:

1. ***Demand Management:*** This is basically co-ordination sales forecasts from all the players, including sales representatives at the point of sale through production to raw material suppliers, so that everyone is working to the same plan, rather than creating unnecessary safety stocks.
2. ***Distribution Resources Planning (DRP):*** This will Keep track of the status of production and procurement of materials for each order, where the goods are located, what transport and warehousing is in use, what stock to keep and when to re-order.
3. ***Transport Management Systems (TMS):*** This kind of subsystem normally keep the information such as :what modes of transport at what cost are available to the shipper; what costs and timings are associated with each route; the order in which to load transport; optimization of multi-segment deliveries; compliance with documentation required for customs and shippers.

4. ***Warehouse Management Systems (WMS):*** These are the systems which are used to optimize the storage and picking of goods in a warehouse, also includes compliance with carrier and customer documentation standards.
5. ***Supplier Relationship Management (SRM):*** This kind of subsystem keeps the information about suppliers of direct and indirect materials, such as agreed terms of trade, records of status, records of contacts between the enterprise and the various points of contact in suppliers.
6. ***Component Supplier Management (CSM):*** Management of lists of preferred suppliers and preferred parts; terms of trade such as delivery and price associated with them; rationalization of existing parts to minimize costs by substituting equivalent parts.

4.2 Technology in SCM

1. *Barcode*

- It was developed by General Telephone and Electronics (GTE) and called KarTrak ACI This scheme involved placing coloured stripes in various combinations on steel plates which were affixed to the sides of railroad rolling stock, which was abandoned after about ten years because the system proved unreliable after long-term use
- A barcode is an optical machine-readable representation of data relating to the object to which it is attached
- Represents data by varying the widths and spacings of parallel lines, and may be referred to as linear or one-dimensional i.e. 1-D
- Later they evolved into rectangles, dots, hexagons and other geometric patterns in two dimensions i.e. 2-D
- They became commercially successful when they were used to automate supermarket checkout systems, a task for which they have become almost universal.

It is highly consistent, which is a very important factor in its efficiency and effectiveness.

2. *RFID*

- Radio-frequency identification (RFID) is the wireless non-contact use of radio-frequency electromagnetic fields to transfer data, for the purposes of automatically identifying and tracking tags attached to objects

- These tags contain electronically-stored information, while tags are powered by and read at short ranges (a few meters) via magnetic fields (electromagnetic induction)
- Use: An RFID tag attached to an automobile during production can be used to track its progress through the assembly line. Pharmaceuticals can be tracked through warehouses. Livestock and pets may have tags injected, allowing positive identification of the animal. On off-shore oil and gas platforms, for example, RFID tags are worn by personnel as a safety measure, allowing them to be located 24 hours a day and to be quickly found in emergencies.

3. *Electronic Data interchange*

- EDI can be formally defined as the transfer of structured data, by agreed message standards, from one computer system to another without human intervention
- In 1996, the National Institute of Standards and Technology defined electronic data interchange as & quot; the computer-to-computer interchange of strictly formatted messages that represent documents other than monetary instruments
- Electronic data interchange (EDI) is an electronic communication system that provides standards for exchanging data via any electronic means
- By adhering to the same standard, two different companies, even in two different countries, can electronically exchange documents (such as purchase orders, invoices, shipping notices, and many others). EDI has existed for more than 30 years, and there are many EDI standards
- EDI implies a sequence of messages between two parties, **either of whom** may serve as originator or recipient
- The formatted data representing the documents may be transmitted from originator to recipient via telecommunications or physically transported on electronic storage media

4. *Artificial intelligence/expert systems*

- It is the intelligence exhibited by machines or software, and the branch of computer science that develops machines and software with intelligence AI researchers and textbooks define the field as "the study and design of intelligent agents & quot;

- The central problems (or goals) of AI research include reasoning, knowledge, planning, learning, linguistic communication, perception and the ability to move and manipulate objects
- The field was founded on the claim that a central property of humans, intelligence- the sapience of Homo sapiens- can be so precisely described that it can be simulated by a machine
- Thus, artificial intelligence/expert systems attempt to replicate human intelligence to a machine.
- These (expert)systems reproduce "best practices" of humans to a computer-based system
- Artificial intelligence has been the subject of tremendous optimism but has also suffered stunning setbacks
- Today it has become an essential part of the technology industry and defines many challenging problems at the forefront of research in computer science

5. *Extensible Markup Language*

- Extensible Markup Language (XML) is a mark-up language that defines a set of rules for encoding documents in a format that is both human-readable and machine-readable
- It is defined in the XML 1.0 Specification produced by the W3C , and several other related specifications, all free- open standards
- The design goals of XML emphasize simplicity, generality, and usability over the Internet
- It is a textual data format with strong support via Unicode for the languages of the world
- Although the design of XML focuses on documents, it is widely used for the representation of arbitrary data structures , for example in web services
- Many application programming interfaces (APIs) have been developed to aid software developers with processing XML data, and several schema systems exist to aid in the definition of XML-based languages
- Thus, it is nothing but a system of stuffing information for movement on the Internet

- Due to the rise in the internet, it has a capability to replace Electronic Data Interchange in the near future

6. *Other technologies*

- RF technology: This technology Uses radio frequency to transmit computer outputs, possibly from an expert system to human operated devices, such as, a forklift. It optimizes quality, efficiency, and accuracy
- Imaging: In this technology,both photographic and facsimile processes are currently being used to image documents
- It is the telephonic transmission of scanned printed material (both text and images), normally to a telephone number connected to a printer or other output device. Then, the original document is scanned with a fax machine (or a tele-copier), which processes the contents (text or images) as a single fixed graphic image, converting it into a bitmap, and then transmitting it through the telephone system
- Onboard computers and satellite tracking:This is nothing but a systems which uses tools such as GPS to track and communicate with mobile and/ or remote vehicles
- GPS is a space-based satellite navigation system that provides location and time information in all weather conditions, anywhere on or near the Earth where there is an unobstructed line of sight to four or more GPS satellites
- There is a subsystem present which carries and stores data between the various electronics units and the ground segment , via the Telemetry, Tracking and Command (TTC) subsystem

4.3 Role of Artificial Intelligence (AI) in agricultural supply chain

The population in the world is expected to growth from 7.7 billion to 9.7 billion by year 2050 according to United Nations. And we are in the global warming effects which cause shortage of the supply in agriculture productions in next few decades. With the advance of digital technologies development, one of the must use in digital technologies to overcome the problem of agriculture supply chain is Artificial Intelligence technology.

This article explores how farmer entrepreneurs can look into the application of artificial intelligence for agriculture supply into areas such as farm production process, distribution, transportation, pricing that can control the consistency of agriculture supply chain effectively.

Understanding Artificial Intelligence

Artificial Intelligence (AI) is a technology that use the simulation of human intelligence processes by 3 subsets component such as Neural networks, Machine learning and Deep Learning. Robotic Process Automation is not part of AI but it can automate the production process without any manpower needed.

Machine Learning is a subset of AI, is enables a system to learn from data rather than through explicit programming. It's uses a variety of algorithms to allow the computers learn automatically without human intervention or assistance and adjust actions accordingly. Machine learning requires right set of data to perform learning. Machine learning algorithm can be categorized into either supervised or unsupervised machine algorithm. Supervised machine algorithm is described in the mathematically where you have put variables (x) into a function to give output (Y), and this is used to learn as mapping functions to let you input different new input data to get the output possible results, Y = f (X). Unsupervised machine algorithm is a machine learning technique that you do not need to supervise the model. This algorithm is used to find all kind of unknown pattern in data to discover interest of relationships between variable in the database.

Deep learning is another subset of AI, its function is to mimic the working of human brain in processing data for use in decision making and also able to learn from the data that is both unstructured and unlabeled which can help to detect fraud.

Agricultural Supply Chain

Many farmers do not have good knowledge about agricultural supply chain. They produce their agriculture products and sell to middlemen where they can only make very marginal profit. In today, farmers can be learning basic knowledge of supply chain which can make their financial improving with provide competitive advantage and serviceability to reach out their consumer and let customer stay loyalty to their brand. Agricultural supply chain includes all process from supplier, farming, processing, distribution, retail and consumer, as shown in the diagram below.

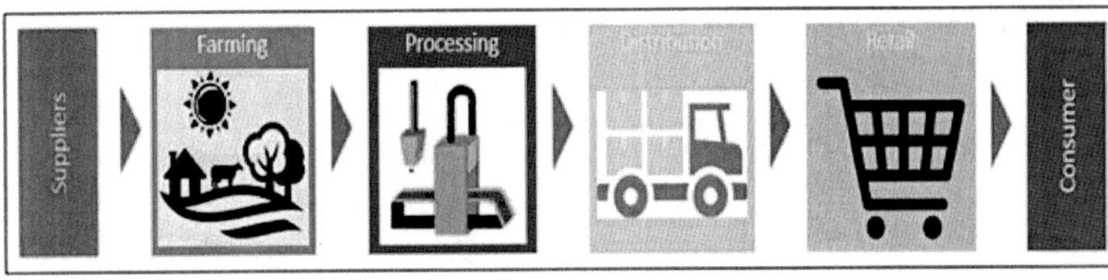

Image taken from https://www.precisionag.com/in-field-technologies/connectivity/iot-will-transform-the-agriculture-supply-chain-get-on-board/

With supply chain knowledge, the business decision to implement Artificial Intelligence involves 4 areas of the supply chain:

1. Supplier management
2. SMART Farming
3. Autonomous Transportation
4. SMART Retail

AI in Supplier Management

With Artificial Intelligence application into supplier management, a single digital procurement platform that consists of supplier management enablers which you can digitalized all supplier information from supplier registration, evaluation, supplier approval, supplier rating, risk and compliance and data analytic.

Supplier Registration, Evaluation and Approval is a basic of procurement to sourcing process which identify the supplier registration from company basic information, financial health check, evaluation to their products and managements system and ensure the approval process is transparency according to company policy in the systems.

- ***Supplier rating, risk and compliance*** become very important in procurement policy where supplier risk management is part of quality management systems process. Supplier can view their rating classification in their logon into buyer procurement systems and their acceptance of risk and compliance term and conditions through digital acceptance.

- ***Data Analytics*** provide effectiveness AI in supervised and unsupervised algorithms which can spot the unusual pattern of relationship of stakeholders and supplier relationships to detect fraud management that not provide good quality of soil nutrients to grow a good healthy agriculture product.

Image taken from https://www.zdnet.com/article/intel-tunes-its-iot-solutions-with-the-help-of-blueberry-farmers/

AI in SMART Farming

With these decades of Industrial 4.0, more IoT chips and sensor was developed with capabilities to provide real time digital data input for agriculture industries to be more effective to control and monitor their production in soil management, water management and plant management. Robotic Processing Automation can be applied in harvesting process be part of data integration with AI agriculture supply chain.

- Soil and Water management can be effectively managed by implant the measuring sensor device that is battery operated that can be wireless connected to cloud technology that provide all real time digital measurement data such as soil moisture, soil temperature and air temperature that give better manage to provide the plants with a healthy environment to growth.AI can make decision to give farmer instruction to do their water management and fertilizing management from the deep learning process.

- Plant management, agriculture drones is developed for better plant management by capturing images of weeds and plants conditions that using AI machine learning algorithms to identify the activation of weed management by laser burning and effectively manage the plants which affect by insects attacked. And as well to monitor the healthiness of growing plants in the big fields which traditionally is impossible to do it in real time decision.

Image taken from https: //howtodrones.com/drone-for-agriculture/remote-sensing-and-precision-agricultural-drones-applications-for-farmers/

AI in Autonomous Transportation

Agriculture Product is a non-durable product which the life cycle is very short less than a week which effective transportation is a crucial in the supply chain process with minimum transportation risk and give accurate real time delivery time to the customer which give good responsive to customer order within the order fulfilment

5

Role of Packaging in Agricultural Supply Chain

5.1 Importance of Agricultural Packaging

As the population of the world rises, there is an increase in the demand for food production. **Agricultural packaging** helps farmers and makers to deliver food in the handiest approach with no loss. It eliminates unnecessary wastage of food during post-harvest treatment procedures, production process, storage, and transportation. It ensures short and long-term stability between the farmers and the consumers. Pesticides are completely toxic and reactive and thus need correct packaging. In agricultural packaging of pesticides, pouches with excellent quality standards are used that improve sealing and handling issues and avoid any malfunctioning. Ventilation is very important in agricultural packaging that permits the warmth and to cool quickly. Loss of water of the products should be minimized to let them stay fresh for a longer time.

Consumers of the agricultural product are today greeted with innovative choices that cut across packaging styles. They say packaging protects against harm or contamination by micro-organisms, air, wetness, and toxins. Agriculturists note that correct packaging prevents product spilling or leaky. Experts observe that the advantages of packaging agricultural product within the sector embrace value, speed, quality, and innovation. The packaging is an important medium for conserving food quality, minimizing food wastage and reducing preservatives used in food. Experts note that packaging plays a vital role in protection against chemical and physical damage while providing information essential to consumers and marketers. Correct packaging enhances the planning, appeal, and feel of your agricultural product and also grabs attention. Adequate packaging helps in advertising and raising the product worth so resulting in higher sales. They also add that it provides customer satisfaction with strong customer oriented approach.

There are several points between where things can go wrong in handling, stacking, and transporting.

Agricultural packaging is important during this sector to stop food from being ruined or spoiled before reaching shoppers. Common agricultural packaging products include bulk bags, silo bags, pouches, clamshells, bottles, trays, and other containers. They are made up of different materials such as plastic, paperboard, glass, jute, and others.

Furthermore, it should be easy to handle, safe to transport, and resistant to injuries and punctures. They help in preserving the quality and integrity of the food. Agricultural packaging has taken on a brand new level of importance considering food is lost after-harvest treatment and storage transportation.

Why is agricultural packaging important?

The packaging inside the agricultural business can facilitate to preserve food. It will also save you money on shipping costs and will aid in product branding. Plus, utilizing the proper agricultural packaging is important in delivering the freshest, best-looking products to your customers.

Bulk bags are suitable for regional and international transport. They have become an industry standard for over a century. These flexible containers are affordable, durable, and reliable. As a result, products arrive in the best possible condition with minimal losses. They are the primary style of packaging used for farm in warehouses before they're distributed in smaller quantities and packages.

Large Scale Use

This packaging choice prices little and can enable customers to ascertain within the package before they go, which can encourage them to make the purchase. Choosing the proper packaging for your products can reduce losses, keep foods fresh, and make them more appealing to consumers. The past few years have seen a new generation of packaging materials that are ecological-friendly and recyclable.

How does packaging boost your agricultural exports?

With the increasing population, food production demand also increases. Agricultural packaging helps farmers and the exporters to deliver food in the handiest approach without any loss. Packaging prevents unnecessary waste post-harvest and during the processes of production, storage and transportation. It ensures short and long-term stability between the farmers and consumers.

- ***Packaging for agricultural export business***: The packaging is rising an essential element for your export operation, impacting the safety, cost, communication and even marketing of your agricultural products.

Agricultural packaging has gained immense popularity across the world. According to Statista, the global agricultural packaging market is expected to reach [$5.02 billion by the end of 2023](https://www.statista.com/statistics/916723/global-agricultural-packaging-market/). If you want your agricultural products to reach different horizons across the world, you should consider the features, importance and benefits of packaging. - Safety of agricultural products - Accurate handling instructions

Importance of packaging in the export business: From the contractual point of view, you are responsible for the packaging of agricultural products such that it withstands the transportation process. If the packaging is damaged in the port of destination, then the handling of the cargo is not considered responsible. Responsibility of seller: According to the new edition of [Incoterms 2010] (https://iccwbo.org/resources-for-business/ incoterms-rules/ incoterms-rules-2010/), the seller will be responsible for any damage happened to the products during the journey.

- ***Security of goods:*** The primary purpose of the agricultural packaging is not limited to protecting the cargo during the international logistic process. The packaging is also an essential element of the product's marketing, as it conveys a strong image of the company in front of the consumers.
- ***Cost saving:*** Packing affects the cost of your products. The packaging must adapt to the cargo units deployed to optimize the use of trucks, containers and the other form of transportation.
- ***Storage and organization:*** Packages end up taking more space when not compatible with pallets and thus, waste up to 20% of the container's space, adding 40% extra cost to in the price of your product.
- ***Handling information:*** The packaging is also essential in terms of the instructions and other handling information. How the carrier, individual and the cargo handle the products will rely on the knowledge of the packaging. The information on the boxes, help the transporters to stack the boxes. The boxes could be stacked upside down, damaging the products when there is no instruction on the packaging.

- ***Packaging and labelling functions:*** In accord with the importance of packaging, the packaging must have these functions to facilitate the transportation process without any hindrance: - Protect your cargo during international logistics - Communicate your brand with the consumers

  - Your essential constitutional element of marketing - Reflects your customer's cultural value - Instruct carriers how the package should be stacked or handled

How does packaging boost your agricultural exports?

1. ***Protection of goods:*** For agricultural goods, protection of products is necessary, and as the exporter, you have to select the right packaging material to prevent damage. You can request samples to test the packing materials and packaging. The packaging should withstand the transportation process. The means of transportation also plays a vital part in packaging as you have to select the material based on the transport used and the distance covered by the transportation company. It is necessary to use different kinds of material to target different markets.
2. ***Business communication:*** The packaging is something that communicates the product's features to its buyers, making it the essential marketing tool for exporters. For agricultural products, you can instruct the consumers about the ingredient or can even warn them about the allergies. Before initiating the export operation, preferences of the consumers in the target market should be assessed to ensure that the package meets the consumer's expectations.
3. ***Indicating the size of the package:*** The agricultural packaging and its material must be optimized to maximize the use of cargo units. The packaging should be designed in a way that a maximum number of packages fit in each box. The size of the boxes should be considered for pallet use. EUR-Pallet is the most commonly used pallet across the world, which measures 1,200mm X 800mm X 144mm, which is approximate to 47.2 inches X 31.5 inches X 5.7 inches. With these dimensions, the exporters can ensure maximum utilization of the space. It would help if you considered these calculations before packing your agricultural products.
4. ***Information for handling:*** The package must indicate how it is handled. The agricultural exporter must mention how the product should be processed on the boxes. They can print indications along with the symbol like "this side up," maximum stacking height," handle with care" and

many others. All these indications should be listed outside the packages so that the carrier can transport them without damaging the products. Besides, it would help if you also considered other indications which are mandatory in your company's product include precautions regarding the exposure to sunlight, damp and extreme temperatures.

5. ***Reflects your customer's cultural values:*** The information on the packaging should reflect your customer's cultural values. No matter where does your customer resides, you should consider the local language and other aspects of the information. In Turkey and Austria, green is well- accepted colour, while in China, red and yellow is accepted because of the royalty in its culture. You should conduct proper cultural analysis before designing your package to ensure and enhance the cultural values of your potential customers. What does this ultimately mean? A right package can not only protect your shipments but also foster sales and increase the perception of value among your customers. Thus, packaging an important aspect which cannot be ignored to boost up the agricultural export across the world.

https://www.freightfarms.com/blog/types-of-crop-packaging clamshells-

Clamshells related to shellfish only in their hinged design, clamshells are a common packaging method for herbs and tender hydroponic lettuces with the roots still attached. Plastic clamshells are great for selling to grocery stores and at farmers markets.

Pros

- The plastic shell of a clamshell does a great job of protecting your crops from being bruised or damaged.
- Clear packaging allows shoppers to easily view your produce and see for themselves how amazing it is.
- The flat surface of the clamshell offers a convenient space for you to display your label — all you need is a branded sticker.
- Plastic keeps the moisture in, so that your product stays fresher longer.
- Most clamshells can be recycled.

Cons

- Plastic, especially for our environmentally-conscious farmers and customers, can be offputting.
- Typically single-use packaging, this means a continual cost for your business.

Compostable Clamshells

Similar in design to plastic clamshells, this is a compostable alternative made from plant-based fibers. Consider using compostable clamshells for selling at farmers markets.

Pros

- The hard shell of the clamshell protects your crops from bruising or damage.
- You can easily mark the packaging with a stamp or sticker for brand visibility.

These clamshells can be recycled and composted Cons

- The fiber material of the clamshell absorbs moisture, which can cause greens to go limp faster than other options.
- An opaque material means that shoppers will not be able to see your product, which is inherently one of your best marketing tools. It is therefore not a great option for markets where customers have choice and do not already know your brand (like supermarkets). If you're selling to sales channels like farmers markets, consider displaying samples of your produce to counter this downside.
- This is single-use packaging.

Plastic Bags

The ubiquitous produce packager, plastic bags are an option that you and your customers will be familiar with. Plastic produce bags are great for all sales channels: farmers markets, grocery stores, CSAs, and even restaurants (depending on the size of the bag).

Pros

- Again, clear packaging allows shoppers to get a look at your produce and see just how delicious and fresh it looks.
- You can easily affix a branded sticker to the outside of the bag.
- On a per-unit basis, plastic bags are the cheapest packaging option you'll find.
- Plastic traps moisture, keeping your produce fresher for longer.
- A variety of plastic bags are available, including those with small perforations for those greens that benefit from more
- breathability.
- Typically sold as a roll, these are convenient and require minimal storage space.

Cons

- Most plastic bags are not recycled.
- This is a single-use packaging method, and therefore an ongoing cost for your business operations.
- While plastic bags do keep your produce fresh, they do not protect delicate leafy greens from being bruised or crushed. To counter this, some farmers make sure to seal their bags with air (like a balloon) for extra cushion.

Compostable Bags

- Typically recognized by their greenish hue or slight opacity, these biodegradable bags are similar in appearance to plastic bags and offer many of the same benefits, but are a more environmentally-conscious option, made from corn-based plastic or a similar plant derivative. Again, these are a great option for farmers markets, grocery stores, CSAs, and restaurants alike.

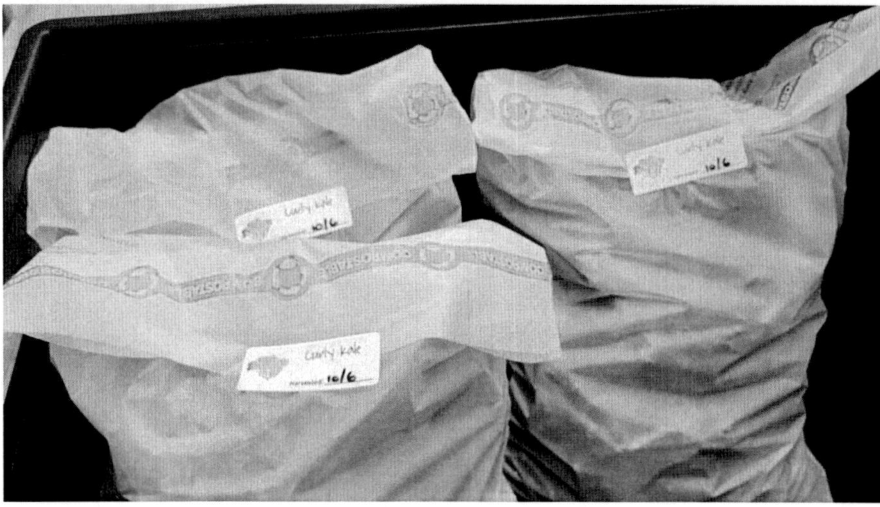

Pros

- Compostable produce bags are a more sustainable option than plastic.
- You can easily label these bags with a sticker for brand visibility.
- While slightly more expensive than plastic, these compostable bags are still a highly cost-effective option.
- Typically sold as a roll, these are convenient and require minimal storage space.

Cons

- Since these bags are slightly tinted and not 100% clear, produce is slightly less visible than it would be in a standard plastic bag.
- Some compostable produce bags can only be composted using industrial methods (not by the backyard composter).
- Some farmers have found that these bags can cause produce to degrade faster than plastic options.

Paper Bags

- A beautifully rustic option, these earthy-looking bags can also contribute to your brand image. Farmers typically only use these for farmers markets or CSAs.

Pros

- Using non-plastic packaging shows your business' dedication to sustainability.
- Paper bags are both recyclable and compostable.
- You can easily label paper produce bags using a sticker or a stamp.
- A stiffer material than plastic, this bag offers some protection from bruising and crushing to your greens.

Cons

- Paper does not preserve your greens as well as some other options. The material absorbs moisture from your plants, and will likely cause your produce to wilt faster than an airtight container or bag.
- Because shoppers cannot see your produce through the paper bag, this is not an ideal option for markets where customers have choice and do not already know your brand (like supermarkets). In customer segments like farmers markets, consider displaying samples of your produce to counter this downside.
- Once again, this is a single-use option.

Bands & Ties

- Perhaps the most minimal packaging there is, rubber bands, twist ties, or knotted twine can be utilized to easily bundle larger leafy greens and herbs still attached to the stalks. Bands and ties are typically used for farmers markets and CSAs.

Pros

- Produce shines in this option, which allows shoppers to see the fullness of your leaves of kale and smell the scent of your sage.
- A highly minimalist packaging option, this produces less packaging waste than other methods.
- For hardy crops like swiss chard and kale, which are stronger and slower to wilt, this packaging presents everything the leaves need and nothing extraneous.

Cons

- Bundling is not viable for all crops. It does not present any protection against wilting, bruising, or tears, so it's not as strong an option for delicate crops such as lettuces. Additionally, smaller leaves such as arugula and spinach cannot be bundled together in this manner.
- It can be harder to label crops when they're bunched together. In order to affix your branding, you'll have to consider something like a dangling tag.
- Produce typically decays faster in the area bound by ties; consumers will have to remove ties to prevent early spoilage.

Bins

Durable plastic bins can be another great bulk packaging option — especially for delivery to restaurants, campus dining halls, wholesalers, and CSA customers.

Pros

- These bins are reusable and will last you a long time.
- You can harvest in bulk without having to individually package small quantities of greens.
- Some bins are collapsible, making for easy storage when not in use.

Cons

- Bins are not a viable packaging option for most customer segments.

Boxes

Cardboard boxes can be a great option for bulk packaging, restaurant deliveries, or CSAs. You may also be able to find small paper boxes that can be used to package smaller portions of crops.

Pros

- Cardboard is ultra-recyclable.
- This saves time and money, since you won't have to worry about individually packaging crops.
- Waxed or plastic-lined cardboard boxes can be reused.

Cons

- Moisture from your crops can make an unlined box soggy, potentially causing it to break.
- In the case of a CSA with a variety of vegetables, delicate greens and herbs won't have protection and could be crushed by other contents of the box.
- A more porous material, cardboard will not prevent your greens from wilting.
- Unless waxed or plastic-lined, this is likely a single-use packaging material.

6

International Organization for Standardization (ISO)

The full form of 'ISO' is the **International Organization for Standardization**. ISO -QMS was founded in the year 1987. Its headquarters are in Geneva, Switzerland, operating in 162 plus countries.

- The ISO is an international standard-setting body that consists of the representatives from various national standards organizations.
- The ISO works on formulating the standards and guidelines for a variety of businesses and other purposes and publishes technical reports.
- The word 'ISO' is derived from the Latin term 'isos' which means 'Equal for everyone'. It simply means that all the elements of the international std are equally applicable to all types of business.

History of ISO

- Modern standardization appeared in the 19th century along with industrialization. At the end of the 19th century, the need for standards became international.
- The development of international standards is the need for acceptance of services and products at the global level. At the same time, at the international level, an international system of units that facilitated technical dialogue was adopted.

Role of ISO

The Role of the international organization for standardization is to bring together experts from various fields to share knowledge, experience and develop consensus-based international standards which support innovation and provide alternatives to solve global challenges. Some of the roles Of ISO are as followed:

- Develops and publishes standards for a larger range of materials, processes, and products

- An established common standard for different countries by facilitating. world trade.
- Ensures that products and services are reliable and safe.

The ISO standards are finalized after an international agreement by experts in related fields.

The experts are the people who are aware of the need of the industries and the other individuals such as manufacturers, sellers, customers, trade associations, buyers, users, and regulators.

Types of ISO standards

Few of the commonly adopted ISO standards are

- **ISO 9001-** This standard deals with the criteria for quality management systems.
- **ISO 14001-** This standard works on providing criteria for environment. Management systems
- **ISO 27001-** This standard specifies the requirements for the establishment, implementation, maintenance, and continuous improvement of information security management systems within the context of the organization.
- **ISO 22000 -** This standard deals with the criteria for Food safety management systems.
- **ISO 45001-** This standard works on providing criteria for occupational health and safety Management systems.

Need For ISO

- ISO is required to identify and describe processes by using business metrics. The main purpose is to provide better management and control of business processes. These goals are present at the core of the system.
- The International Organization for Standardization (ISO) is an international standard setting body. The organization promulgates worldwide proprietary, industrial, and commercial standards.
- ISO is the world's leading developer and publisher of standards. In addition to quality standards, ISO helps companies across the globe to have commonly acceptable standards to ensure trade promotion between two nations on consistent basis.

ISO 9000

ISO 9000 is a set of international standards on quality and quality assurance developed to help companies effectively document the quality management system elements to be implemented to maintain an efficient quality control system. They are not specific to any industry and can be applied to any organization.

Scope of ISO 9000

ISO 9000 can help a company satisfy its customers, meet regulatory requirements and achieve continual improvement. However, it should be considered to be a first step, the base level of a quality control system and not a complete guarantee of quality control.

ISO 9000 is most widely known and has perhaps had the most impact among various standards published by ISO.

It serves many different industries and organizations as a guide to quality of products, services and managements. An organization can be ISO 9000 certified if it successfully follows the ISO 9000 standards for its industry.

ISO 9000 deals with the fundamentals of quality management systems, including the management principles, upon which the family of standards is based. ISO 9000 was first published in 1987. It was based on the BS 5750 series of standards from BSI that was proposed to ISO in 1979.

Management Principles of ISO 9000 Family of Standards

1. ***Customer Focus Organization:*** Organizations depend on their customers for existing in the business and therefore should understand current and future customers' needs, should meet customers' requirements and strive to exceed customers' expectations.

2. ***Leadership:*** Leadership is very important in any organization to be successful. Without clear and strong leadership, a business flops. Proper leadership is essential for the direction of the organization.

3. ***Involvement of People:*** People's involvement is very crucial. An organization is nothing without its staff whether part time, full time, in house or outsourced. It is their abilities that help maximize business success.

4. ***Process Approach:*** The process approach is all about efficiency and effectiveness. It is also about consistency and understanding that good

processes also speed up activities. Great processes reduce cost, improve consistency, eliminate waste and promote continuous improvement.

5. ***Systematic Approach to Management:*** To increase an organization's effectiveness and efficiency in achieving its objectives, it should identify, understand and manage interrelated processes as a system.

   The organization should establish quality policy and quality objectives to provide a focus and direction to the organization.

6. ***Continual Improvement:*** Organization should maintain current levels of performance. It ought to respond to the changing conditions and circumstances. An organization must identify, create and exploit new opportunities when they establish and sustain ongoing focus on improvement.

7. ***Factual Approach to Decision Making:*** Efficient decisions are based on the analysis of data and information. Appropriate decisions, based on experience and entrepreneurial intuition can only be reached when these data and information are reviewed and verified continuously.

8. ***Mutually Beneficial Organization and Supplier Relationship:*** Everything is interdependent. Organizations particularly depend on good business relationships with their suppliers. This is the only way for parties to make the maximum contribution to the creation of mutual value and mutual trust. Good consistent supplier performance help companies to achieve their goals on regular basis.

ISO 9001

ISO 9001 is one of the standards within the range of ISO 9000 standards. ISO 9001 is a set of internationally agreed standards that provide guidelines for quality management systems (QMS). ISO 9001 is a document which outlines the criteria or requirements of QMS. ISO 9001 sets out the preconditions that an organization must maintain in its quality control system. ISO 9001 was first published in 1987 by ISO. Its QMS gradually evolved up to present time.

The following are the ISO 9001 standards versions released from start till date.

- ISO 9001:1987,ISO 9001:1994,ISO 9001:2000, ISO 9001:2008 and ISO 9001:2015

Functions of ISO 9001

ISO 9001:2015 is the current and latest version of ISO 9001. The main functions of ISO 9001 are to set out the criteria for QMS and also to provide the basic standards for certification of any organization. It can be used by all kinds of organizations, whether large or small, regardless of their activities. In fact, there are over one million companies and organizations in over 170 countries certified to ISO 9001.

ISO 9001 QMS are voluntary and not mandatory upon any organization. ISO 9001 just lays out the requirements of QMS which are open to any organization to adopt. ISO 9001:2015 QMS is a document consisting of 10 clauses .

Purpose ISO 9001

- The main objective of ISO 9001 is to provide an organization the quality control system that will provide the foundation to better customer satisfaction, staff motivation and continual improvement.
- ISO 9001 certification provide maximum benefit to an organization if the organization implements the QMS in a practical way. By adopting QMS of ISO 9001, an organization can start to implement more efficient working practices and can focus more on its business objectives.

Certification

- ISO certification is given through certification bodies. Numerous certification bodies exist, which audit organizations and upon success, issue ISO compliance certificates. ISO 9001 certified means an organization has met the requirements of ISO 9001.
- ISO certification is valid for three years from the date of issue, subject to successful compliance of the same in every year surveillance audit.
- The Following Procedure Must be Followed to Obtain ISO 9001 Certification

Commit to get ISO 9001 Certification

To obtain ISO 9001 certification a commitment and a fair decision from the top management or the decision maker is essential.

An Appointment of Internal Project Manager

The organization needs someone to oversee things internally. Getting the third party certification is a project. So, it should be treated as a project. Research should be done to find a consulting partner to do the handholding.

Allocate Resources

Getting ISO 9001 certification involves time, effort and expenditure. Therefore, the organization must allocate fund and assign employees for the achievement of the same.

1. ***Establishment of Baseline Status:*** The organization must find out where they are as of date w.r.t. goals set by the management or its baseline. The organization should identify how much gap it has to fill out and how much improvement it has to make to be eligible for certification.
2. ***Development of the System***: After the gap analysis, the organization must develop its quality control system. In most cases it may mean improving the existing condition by filling up the gaps. If necessary, the organization ought to develop new processes, procedures, quality control systems or even documentation. An organization should make all the changes or improvement necessary to fulfill the requirements of the standards related to documented information compliance.
3. ***Auditing the System***: The organization must internally audit their own system i.e. compliances and risks audit and not financial audit. The organization should conduct internal audit to check that its performance and activities matches with the system and requirements including the ISO 9001 requirements. When any problems or weaknesses are found then the organization should fix them with its own formal processes that exist in its own system.
4. ***Selecting an External Auditor***: An accredited auditor, registrar or certifier should be chosen by making a formal application and by paying the prescribed fees. The date of certification audit must be arranged and scheduled.
5. ***To have the External Audit***: The external certifier will audit the organization's quality management system against all the requirements of ISO 9001. It is a rigorous test for the organization's team to demonstrate their capability against the set target.
6. ***Scope of the Certification***: If the organization becomes successful in the test, the certifier will award the coveted certificate to the organization. In the certificate it generally mentions the scope of the certificate and what it covers. In case of ISO 9001, the certifier will insert the name of the company, location covered, and activities involved with certification. Thereafter, the organization will be able to claim that it has ISO 9001 certification or ISO 9001 registration.
7. ***Maintaining the Certificate***: Each certification is awarded for a three-year period. During this period the company can continue to run the system, maintain it and of course improve it. From time to time the internal auditor will come and check the compliance as per plan. At the end of three years, certification body will come for full audit and for re-certification.

Benefits of having International Organization for Standardization (ISO) certification include:

1. Improved customer confidence
2. Reduced risk of product and service defects
3. The reduced cost associated with corrective actions.
4. Enhanced reputation and brand image

ISO certification is a process by which an organization can demonstrate compliance with ISO standards. ISO certification assures customers, business partners, and the public that the organization meets internationally recognized quality management system requirements.

Some of the benefits of ISO certification include.

1. Increased customer confidence assures an organization meets internationally recognized quality assurance requirements. This reassures customers that their products or services are of the highest quality on consistent basis.
2. Improved business relationships: ISO certification can benefit businesses in numerous ways. For example, it can improve customer confidence and increase sales volume. It can also lead to new business opportunities as customers seek out suppliers that have been certified.
3. Improved efficiency: When an organization is certified to adhere to ISO standards, it can operate more efficiently and effectively. This leads to cost savings and improved product development and delivery performance.

Requirements to Obtain a Certification in India

To become certified in India, a business must meet certain requirements.

1. The business must have compliance with all the applicable legal requirements of the business.
2. The business must have documented information as per the requirements of the ISO 9001 std.
3. The business must demonstrate sound management practices and meet industry standards (management commitment to quality, system development process, etc.).
4. The business must carry out an on-site audit to ensure compliance with all. certification criteria.

Key points for successful implementation

1. The organization should have a sound quality management system in place.
2. The QMS must be documented and approved by an independent auditor.
3. Each process has targets and reporting system.
4. The audited system must be monitored and maintained on an ongoing basis.

How is ISO Certification Important

ISO certification is important because it ensures that a company or product meets international quality and safety standards. ISO certification can be beneficial to businesses in a number of ways. For example, ISO certification can help improve customer trust and satisfaction, attract new customers, and improve business reputation. Additionally, ISO certification can help reduce manufacturing costs, improve product quality, and increase sales.

Which Countries Have ISO Certifications?

ISO certification is mandatory for any organization that wishes to do business in a country with an ISO code. ISO codes are assigned to countries based on their economic and political stability. The following countries have ISO certifications:

1. United States of America
2. Canada
3. European Union
4. Switzerland
5. Japan
6. Australia
7. New Zealand
8. Israel
9. Singapore
10. Thailand

ISO certification ensures that the quality of products and services exported from these countries is consistent with international standards and best practices. Organizations that hold an ISO certification can be confident that their products will be accepted by consumers and businesses worldwide.

ISO certification also allows organizations to improve their operations by taking advantage of international best practices and standards. An organization can improve its credibility, efficiency, and financial stability by obtaining an ISO certification.

How Can ISO Help the Indian Market?

- ISO certification is one of the most important tools for businesses in India.
- ISO ensures that products and services meet international quality standards, which can improve customer satisfaction and help businesses gain a competitive edge. ISO also ensures that processes are followed correctly, reducing the risk of business failure. Additionally, ISO certification can help businesses attract foreign investment and expand into new markets.
- International Organization for Standardization (ISO) certification is becoming increasingly important as businesses expand into new markets.
- With over 1.3 billion people living in India, there's a lot of potential for growth for businesses with ISO certification.
- Not only will your business operate in a much larger market, but you will also be able to trust your products and services to be treated with the utmost respect.
- ISO certification assures you that your goods are being produced according to international standards and guarantees consistency of performance.

7

G.K. Enterprise ISO 9001: 2015 QMS for Business Improvements

G K Enterprise –Profile in brief

- Established in 2000 to provide Management Consultancy to all types of industries
- Centrally Located in Mumbai
- Consists of Group of Engineers having Industry Experience of more than 20 years
- Completed more than 500 plus ISO Certifications all over India & abroad.
- Certifications done for following areas –manufacturing, service, Education, Medical and projects business
- Established with a purpose of improving work efficiency of all types of business in India & abroad.

Services Offered

- ISO Consultancy Contract from Concept to Certification for 9001/ 14001/ 45001/20000/22000/22301/27001/TS16949/50001/13485 Management Systems
- Internal Audit
- Process Audit
- Performance audit
- Energy Audit
- Internal Auditor Training
- ISO Training Courses
- M.R. training

- Business Risk Audits
- Job Profit Analysis
- Engineering inspection and supplier audits

ISO Certifications and applicability

Standard	Description	Industry
ISO 9001	Quality Management System	ALL
ISO 14001	Environmental Management System	ALL
ISO 45001	Occupational Health & Safety Management System	Healthcare
ISO 20000	Information Technology Service Management System	IT Services
ISO 22000	Food Safety Management System	Food
ISO 22301	Business Continuity Management System	ALL
ISO 27001	Information Security Management System	ALL
ISO 50001	Energy Management System	ALL

What is ISO 9001?

- International Organization for Standardization.
- Basic principle –Defect prevention
- Started in 1987 to promote international trade.
- Accepted in more than 100 plus countries.
- Head office at Geneva-Switzerland
- Used for increasing the effectiveness and efficiency of organization.
- Controls rework, rejection, and wastage
- Certification is valid for three years.
- Consistency is reviewed periodically by third parties.
- Scope of work and locations will be highlighted on the certification.
- As a third-party certification, customers all over the world can view your certificate from the Web site of the international certification body.

How ISO Certification Adds value?

- Every business is established with an aim of achieving excellence in the field of operation and profit in the fastest possible time.

- To ensure both the above elements one needs to increase the sales and improve the operational system on a consistent basis using the system approach and implementation of the Management system.
- ISO ensures distribution of roles and reporting system for management.
- With internal audits one can monitor the company performance on regular basis and management review the same for decision making.
- The company is more system driven and less person based so that performance is not based on individuals.
- Management is expected to take decisions on improvement projects so that there is consistency of growth

Why Business is ISO Certified

- Market demands
- To be eligible for international association
- To get an opportunity to do business with blue chip companies.
- For international courses as a part of requirement
- To ensure system works rather than person-based approach.
- To get the operational controls and improve efficiency.
- To have reputation in the society
- Improve profits.
- To have internationally reputed companies for campus interviews

What are the points management need to know?

- Business data in terms of products and services offered.
- Pricing of products and services, place to do business and method of promotions
- Expected profit margins for each product and service.
- Analysis of expected and actual profit margins
- Overhead costing sheet for the company
- What is the operation cost per product and service?
- What are the business risks one is likely to face
- Mitigation plan to cover risk and achieve improvements.

What are the costing factors for operations?

1. Cost of marketing, sales, and promotion
2. Cost of infrastructure
3. Cost of legal compliance to operate.
4. Cost of manpower salary from management to workers
5. Cost of machines and test instruments-LAB
6. Cost of material –raw material, packing material and consumables
7. Cost of maintenance of equipment, tooling, and critical spares
8. Cost of calibrations and software validations
9. Cost of outsourced processes—job work, transportation, calibration LAB testing
10. Cost of manpower selection and training
11. Cost of rework and rejection and wastage
12. Cost of inventory and material distribution
13. Cost of Staff retention
14. Cost of overhead
15. Cost for availability of finance
16. Cost of safety

How ISO can improve operations

- ISO std. ensures publicity to international level and gives eligibility for all tenders and supplier registration there by reducing cost for promotions and marketing.
- It ensures periodic performance evaluation of all sections to achieve. consistency of performance
- Cost of infrastructure can be calculated, and life cycle assessment will help. long term uninterrupted operations
- Compliance with legal requirements will ensure no disturbance and additional. Costing for statutory visits
- ISO helps to define all legal needs and monitor them as a regular part. of implementation

10 Benefits of ISO 9001.

1. ***Improved chance of winning contracts:*** Having ISO 9001 certification can go a long way to helping a business to secure partnerships with both the public and private sectors. With public sector tenders, certification to ISO 9001 is a strong signal that a business is well-run and credible, removing the need for extensive due diligence. Similarly, many private sector organizations have made it a requirement for their suppliers to be certified to ISO 9001. It signifies that quality is taken seriously and can be relied on in all aspects of the business.

2. ***Higher customer satisfaction***: One of the most important aspects of the ISO 9001 standard is tracking customer satisfaction and responding to any issues raised. Companies that seek and maintain ISO 9001 certification prove that they take this issue seriously.

3. ***Reduced product or service problems***: ISO 9001 certified businesses are better prepared to deal with the unexpected. For instance, if a product is not up to scratch, there will be processes in place that help to ensure that the problem is dealt with efficiently and does not recur.

4. ***Better management***: Appropriate analysis and reporting are key factors in running a business well. The ISO 9001 standard helps businesses to get this right.

5. ***Increased consistency in business practices***: Implementing the practices required by the standard will offer the type of consistency that benefits everyone, including customers. It ensures that processes within a business are common and understood, which helps employees be clearer about the tasks involved, rather than spending time thinking about what to do or having proper work distribution.

6. ***Enhanced employee satisfaction and job security:*** Staff enjoy greater job satisfaction and feel more secure about their jobs in a business where processes are well-defined and clearly managed.

7. ***Lower costs***: Achieving and maintaining certification to ISO 9001 can lead to lower insurance premiums. This is because insurers recognize that these businesses have appropriate processes and controls that reduce risks.

8. ***Streamlined business processes***: No business wants unnecessary paperwork and yet many are burdened by precisely that. The discipline inherent in the ISO 9001 standard means that business processes should be streamlined. Regular reviews mean that processes should not become flabby.

9. ***Continual improvement***: A good quality management system provides a solid foundation for improvements to be made year on year.
10. ***Overall business improvement***: The aggregate effect of the nine individual benefits outlined above is an overall business improvement and consequently profit.

Whether you've been considering ISO 9001 certification for some time, or you are researching it for the first time, we are certain you would see many of these benefits realized once you have implemented the requirements for ISO 9001 certification.

If you're unsure what is required to achieve certification or you are looking for help in achieving it, you should contact us for a no-obligation discussion about your options. Whatever level your needs are we have a solution that is likely to suit your requirements.

Introduction-ISO 9001 2015 QMS

In this std following verbal forms are used – ''Shall ''indicates a requirement.

''Should' indicates a recommendation.

''May ''indicates permission.

''Can ''indicates a possibility or capability.

Quality Management Principles ISO 9001: 2015

1. Customer focus
2. Leadership
3. Engagement of people
4. Process approach
5. Improvement
6. Evidence based decision making.
7. Relationship management

1. ***Customer focus***: Customer focus is key to the mission of quality management. Without loyal customers, businesses can't stay afloat, which is why customer satisfaction should be the goal of every business's quality management system.

   Gathering customer feedback can help a company identify areas where your business can improve, creating a positive cycle of feedback and improvement. Higher customer satisfaction also means more sales and greater profits, improving the business's bottom line.

2. ***Leadership***: If the leaders of a business don't believe in quality management or don't make it a strategic priority, then the quality management initiatives will fail. That's why leadership is the second principle of quality management laid out in ISO 9001. Dedication to quality management must come from the top of the organization.

   Strong leadership means that supervisors are setting the organization's goals for quality management and creating a culture of quality from the top-down. Without a strong vision for quality management from leaders (not to mention a budgetary commitment), businesses will fall short of their quality management goals.

3. ***Engagement of people***: Engagement of people refers to having employees at every level of the organization who are committed to meeting the company's quality management standards and delivering goods or services that result in a high level of customer satisfaction.

   Because entry-level and mid-level employees are the ones responsible for executing the quality management directives, getting them on board is extremely important for carrying out quality management strategies and implementing quality management systems. If leadership covers the "top- down" portion of quality management, then engagement of people is the "bottom-up" portion of creating a culture of quality.

4. ***Process approach***: Process approach refers to seeing a business as a series of interconnected processes rather than separate departments or silos. It means focusing on the dynamic business processes rather than individual positions, team divisions, and other static elements.

   This process approach encourages efficiency, contributes to better resource management, and helps support continuity when team members move on and have to be replaced. When combined, all of these factors contribute to better quality management and also a more flexible business that can respond quickly to market changes.

5. ***Improvement***: Companies never "arrive" or fully achieve their goals when it comes to quality management. Instead, they must reject complacency and be engaged in an ongoing focus on improvement, which is what this principle refers to. When they achieve one quality management goal, companies who are serious about quality management will simply create another, more far-reaching target, so the metaphorical goalposts are always moving.

This focus on continual improvement also helps companies to stay competitive and continue delivering goods and services that satisfy customers. Customers will take their business to the companies that are continuing to improve, so companies must focus on pushing their standards for customer success.

6. ***Evidence-based decision-making***: Evidence-based decision-making means making decisions based on facts, data, and observation rather than unsupported assumptions. Fortunately, quality management software allows companies to make evidence-based decisions quickly.

   While there will always be some level of uncertainty when it comes to setting business strategies, following an evidence-based approach will help reduce the levels of uncertainty and give business leaders more confidence in the accuracy of their decisions.

   This is related to quality management because more accuracy in business decisions translates to higher quality goods and services and in turn, better customer satisfaction.

7. ***Relationship management***: If relationship management sounds more relevant to sales than to quality management, think again. Quality management requires maintaining healthy relationships with all stakeholders—not only customers, but also suppliers, vendors, and distributors as well.

Just because these third-party partners are not technically part of a company does not mean that their actions aren't going to impact that company's ability to meet its quality goals and satisfy its customers. Cultivating strong

relationships with these outside partners and getting them to understand the vision for quality management is key to achieving quality goals.

Ready to get serious about quality management at your company?

1. ***Scope***: All the requirements are generic and applicable to any company regardless of type, size or products and services it provides.

   This std. Specifies requirements for QMS when company needs to demonstrate its ability to consistently provide products and services that meets customer and statutory and regulatory requirements and aims to enhance customer satisfaction through effective use of system and processes.

2. ***Normative reference***: ISO 9000:2015 Quality management systems – Fundamentals and vocabulary.

3. ***Terms and Definitions***: For the purpose of this document the terms and definition given in ISO 9000:2015 apply

Understanding the organization and its context

Shall define internal and external issues relevant to its purpose which affects ability to intended results of QMS

Shall monitor and review information about internal and external issues.

- Every business family, private or public has internal and external issues which.
- Directly impact their ability to serve and provide products as per the target set.
- Each business is set with some purpose of profit earning and also creating value and brand image for sustaining profitability.
- To know your business better one has to go in depth to understand the issues who can impact business in significant way. Internal issues are linked with employees and other groups in contract basis
- External issues are linked with statutory and legal agencies
- One of the common factors will be to get maximum returns on investment!! Which could be in the form of time spent, efforts, finance and other points like knowledge applied and may more.
- How this will be possible? To have this practically achievable one has to plan the business in such a way that all the activities done for all the processes are effective and efficient all the time.
- Now for any business is quality important? answer is very simple no business can survive without it. Is environment in which the work is done will affect the quality and working in general? Is health of employees and safety in working linked to productivity ?
- Many times people understand the linkage but fail to establish mathematical model from the same.
- All business teams submit their offer for products or services they supply with certain basic reason – to have calculated profit /to get the entry in the company or blue-chip client/to ensure operations are on for covering the basic expenses of the company.
- One may not account profitability for cases where entry is needed or to cover basic expense for a cause but majority of the times we find that there is a big margin between expected profit and actual profit due to

many of the following reasons and if you do not bridge this gap as early as possible then it can cause serious issues for the business.

Reasons for dip in profitability

- Estimated manhours and actual manhours needed for job completion are different due to reworking of the job –e.g. one purchase requirement against the customer order is partly fulfilled by the supplier due to reason of his own then what can go wrong—
- Material delivery is in parts for every part delivery inspection team has to carry inspection more no of times then otherwise, store team has to do material handling more times than expected, purchase has to remind /reissue the order to another supplier and accounts will have to deduct TDS more no of times and make payment for more times which could easily result in extra manhours for which customers are not going to pay.
- Another example of rework could be due to mistakes made by the production team resulting in reworking of the product this can be due to lack of competency of team, training not followed, safety not considered or process SOP not followed as per the requirements, which means the same has to be either rejected or replaced which will add working for purchase, production, Quality and stores and dispatch team which customer will not pay and can even result in loss of order or reputation.
- Reworking can also occur due to damaged packing, non-submission of test reports and also due to equipment defects not noticed in time.
- Many companies even do not think about such detailing as they consider it as routine part of the working and finally loss in profit per each order gets them in financial crises, ISO principles if followed to the extent possible can help you to reduce this gap considerably.
- Once we understand above issues it is possible to focus on needs and expectations of interested parties to run the business smoothly. Many times we do not think beyond our resource, knowledge and capability which are key drivers for any business, but failing to judge impact of external and internal issues can be costly as it can give unwanted interruptions and cause problems.
- Once we know what are the issues then we must also have mitigation plan made to reduce the adverse impact of them on our business.
- While making business plan, it is important to note the levels of importance and probability of risk each issue can cause on a long term basis.

- In many businesses people spend more on settling with govt and private agencies due to lack of knowledge on compliances alone, however all successful business empires across the world have few things in common— they are generally legally compliant, have followed labour laws of the land and also keep their suppliers of material and infrastructure happy and growing and it is necessary to follow them if you want to be one of them.

  e.g. Company in the business of hazardous chemical manufacturing operates without pollution control board Licence can have closure notice from them as a surprise gift.

  e.g. Company whose production is manpower driven hires a child labour or deviates from labor laws can result in lockout due to lack of manpower.
- One can easily find that each clause of all the ISO std is linked to effectiveness and efficient working of the business provided we make efforts to understand and implement the same in true spirit.
- We will try our level best to explain the same in coming chapters so that business owners can apply them and improve their profitability on continual basis.
- Understanding the needs and expectations of the interested parties
- Shall determine interested parties that are relevant to QMS
- Shall determine requirements of the interested parties that are relevant to QMS
- Shall monitor and review information about interested parties and their requirements
- Each business has to identify who are the interested parties and how they contribute to the success of the business operations.
- Ref list of interested parties for e.g. and define your own for better understanding and use of the std for performance improvement.
- Interested parties may change with time and also there requirements with the volume of business expansion.
- When business is growing based on the change in the requirements from the customer it is necessary to upgrade the capacity and capability of the loyal suppliers to provide services and material to ensure uninterrupted supply and improve performance.

- Growth is possible only when we start identifying requirements from existing as well as new customers for products and services we provide as a part of contract and develop capacity of our key suppliers in line with the growth in demand.
- Needs are many times defined in terms of laws of the land or part of contract but understanding expectations need specific study and knowledge as that can be governing factor for success.
- Management or owner has to define a time line for knowing when there is change in the interested party e.g. business is expanding to new locations or having new product lines interested party will change as company in engineering product plans a diversion in food items obviously the requirements and interested party both will change.
- Company doing business in INDIA goes to Europe then all or part of the interested party and their requirements need to be reviewed to be successful on consistent basis.
- Owner needs to decide to study /monitor the information about interested party and the extent to which their requirements are fulfilled so that business is sustainable.
- Determining the scope of the Quality management system Shall determine the boundaries and applicability of QMS Shall consider internal and external issues
- Requirements of relevant interested parties referred the products and services of the organization Shall apply all the requirements of the std if applicable within the scope of QMS
- Scope shall be available and maintained as documented information
- Scope shall state types of products and services covered and justification if any requirement is not applicable
- One has to plan for QMS as a part of business expansion method as no other means or ways can give you the kind of recognition you get from the receipt of ISO certification as it is accepted as a token of your commitment towards meeting customer requirements on a consistent manner.
- ISO certificate can give you market platform of entry in more than 200 countries and entry point for business opportunities with many blue chip companies, it can also help you qualify for many tenders across the globe where ISO is considered as one of the qualification criteria to be able to submit the offer.

- While indicating the scope of certification it is necessary to apply your mind to ensure that all the products and services you provide have all the issues defined and requirements of all the interested parties considered so that you are able to achieve continual improvements in the business.

Quality management system and its processes

- Shall establish, implement, maintain and continually improve QMS as per std. Every business when involves more manpower one has to be clear in the expected output of the product and service we intend to deliver to the customer has a fare amount of consistency for being acceptable at all the levels and all the time.
- Establishment of QMS is focused towards documentation part as that is needed to follow a certain sequence and method in working activities ranging from sales to delivery.
- How one can check if the documentation established is effective – simple!!! it can lead the company to achieve the goals set and more importantly change in people do not affect the business.
- Implementation means ensuring what is written is respected by all at all the time and results are accurately defined and achieved as intended by the business owners.
- Good documentation if not used properly will not give good results. e.g. picture of operator not following safety can ruin the business
- Maintain part of QMS is towards consistency of performance so that even if people have changed product operations and service quality is not affected.
- Preservation of key information and usage of the same at any given time when required is linked to maintenance of QMS.
- Loss of key information can bring the business to a standstill and many times this is realized when the impact is seen and no action is possible. e.g. Vehicle taking material has lost customer address and contact.
- Every business is set to earn more profit to increase wages, reputation to gain more business without extra expense on advertising, brand value to get good price as they grow old and hence it is must to have plan for improvements.
- Shall determine the processes needed for QMS and their application throughout the organization Every business has a set of processes to be followed to supply products or provide services to the customers. One

has to know the business cycle which is formed by logical inclusion of all processes.

- Draw your own business cycle and also define list of processes you have to supply products and services. sales, purchase, production, Quality, store delivery etc.
- Shall determine the inputs required and output expected from these processes Each process will have input and output required to perform all the activities of the process. e.g. Purchase process has following activities
- Collect requirements from production and other section for purchase through indent. Identify suppliers for the same and place orders to them
- Ensure material and service acceptance as per the one indicated in PO/ WO
- Do performance rating of key suppliers for consistency and take decision to add or modify the supplier list accordingly.
- One has to know that input of one activity can be output of other as accuracy of acceptance norm, time and qty details in indent as proper input will directly get measured after receipt of material and it's inspection before use.
- Shall determine sequence and interaction of these processes
- Now for purchase process there has to be sequence between material request to release of order, receipt of material, acceptance by quality and then storage at stores or issue to production as per requirements—there has to be interaction between purchase and finance for release of payment, with quality for material inspection, stores for storage and production for further operations Shall determine and apply the criteria and methods needed to ensure effective operation and control of these processes—now in this case criteria for effective operation could be timely procurement of correct qty and quality material and control for that will be indent details, inspection norms, storage norms and payment norms for the operation to be effective.
- Shall determine resources needed for these processes and ensure availability
- Now in above example for a person to handle purchase function effectively will need resources in terms of proper documentation, team to handle the work, software if necessary, finance in time for payment as per PO

terms, inspection team norms of acceptance, storage conditions, and production area for operation, similar resources will be needed for each of process activity which need to be identified and provided for effective outputs.

- Shall assign the responsibilities and responsibilities for these processes

  Is it necessary to give responsibility to all ? Many companies ask such questions during implementation of the system but they never ask is every staff required to give salary or money for working? How people can work without knowing what to do and for what they are responsible?

  Each person in the business belong to certain process or processes in case of multitasking and need to carry task or activity they are responsible for in a defined manner if the output expected is to have certain valid results.

- Shall address the risks and opportunities for the process

  Each process has list of activities as indicated in above example and for all activities if not done properly risk is unavoidable and if done as per norms can also create opportunities.

  In order to understand risk one has to be aware of the impact of the activity or task on process and on business.

- In this case, if a key raw material is not made available in time and of required qty., it can stop production and can delay delivery of finished product to the customer causing loss of reputation, can cause penal action and loss of business and also be linked to delay of payment from the client due to delay in supply as possible effects or risk .
- Now if the same purchase is for stationery item which is for stock purpose then terms of risk will change to great extent, so it is important to identify correct risk so as to classify them and make mitigation plan for reduction in the risk .
- In the same example if material procurement is done as per plan, then can create opportunity to get production in time, delivery in time, payment and possible new business from the customers.
- One has to identify all possible risks and opportunities for all processes and activities within the process to be able to classify them and prepare action plan to reduce risk and increase opportunities.
- This activity is very important as all of us will agree that one who can manage The risk and create more opportunity will have better success in the business.

- Shall evaluate these processes and implement the changes needed to achieve intended results One must know how to evaluate the process ? Can be through process target achievement or through defining control parameters for key activities .
- In this example purchase process can be evaluated by noting no of indents complied as per requirements or through ratio of timely delivery of each consignment as per PO terms.
- When do we need to implement changes ?if process target is not achieved due to any reason Shall Improve the process and QMS
- In QMS every process need to be improved to improve company performance Shall maintain documented information to support operation of its processes Why we need to have documented information?
- One need not reinvent the wheel while the process related activities are on.
- We can use the information to understand where things went wrong and can take timely actions to avoid repetition of mistakes that can impact our business. Shall retain documented information that processes are carried as planned
- This is needed to confirm that operations and planning are in line with the business needs.

Records related to clause 4

1

- Internal and external issue sheet
- Monitor objectives and review through management review meeting

2.

- List of interested parties.
- Interested party requirement sheet.
- Monitor objectives and review through management review meeting

3. Scope of QMS for the company

List of processes and overall process flow chart

- Process block diagram covering inputs and outputs.
- Process operation and planning

Case study-Indicate correct /wrong/may be possible

1. External issues are defined by top management and circulated in board meeting
2. External issues may not cover issues related to culture
3. Internal issues are defined by workers and staff approved by board
4. Organization is paying amount to settle the govt official is a monitoring tool for review of ext issue
5. In internal issue ther is no performance goal covered
6. Provision of knowledge beyond syllabus is internal issue
7. Parents and guardians are interested party
8. External service provider for housekeeping is the interested party
9. Requirement of handicap students is to be considered as part of requirements of interested party
10. Alumni is interested party
11. Board reviews and monitor interested party requirements through details of exam results and job opportunities
12. Monitoring and review of int party is by knowing fees collected and tax paid
13. Scope of certification is discussed in the board meeting but not displayed
14. Part time courses are not covered in the scope of the EOMS as they are small part of the revenue.
15. EOMS Process does not cover outsourced part of the process
16. There is no interaction needed of sport process with the canteen process
17. Process SOP/WI not available for housekeeping and HR related activity/ process
18. Process operation team not aware of the changes they need to maintain as they are responsible for working as per norms.
19. Process outputs are not measurable for support functional process
20. Responsibility and authority for process not assigned by top management but given by process head.

Exercise -Process for Admission

S. No.	Points to follow	Details
1	Inputs --needed and source of information admission formsreceipt book payment modes eligibility criteria background checking	types of courses college norms for reservation
2	Output or the target of the process	correct admission as per normtimely completion of process
3	Step by step approach for theprocess -sequence	100% accuracy of payment andadmissions given SOP/WI for distribution of forms payment collection
4	Interaction with other processes	Verification of documentcanteen facility housekeeping
5	Performance indicators of process	Account office 100% as per norms 100% accurate for payment collection 100% as per time specified Make demo PPT for entire process as a part of training kit
6	Resources needed--man.equipment or machine, information and material	manpower, ATM, NEFT facility, college rule book, printed material, ID cards
7	Responsibility and authority team involved in the process	responsibility for distribution of form-online and physical authority to accept application andgive admission responsibility for communication towards documentsubmission communication on college rules and regulations
8	Risk and opportunity linked to process	admission to non competent students admission without verification of documents as per UGC norm too much time can result in loss ofcandidates management can plan strategy based on empty seats

9	Process evaluation methods	before admission --through dummy entry during the admission through random sample after the process throughperformance indicators
10	Process improvements	reduce the process time ensure accuracyin accounting
11	Process documentation kit and training	Entire list for admission process -check list and records for proof of admission define minimum competency needed forthe activity time period needed for each admission records to be stored --physical and softcopy Make demo PPT for entire process as a part of training kit

ISO CLAUSE 4.0

Ref.	Shall of the std.	Documented information	plan changes	detailsneeded
4.1	determine Ext and int issuesmonitor and review information for ext. and int issue	mission andvision statement	if issueschange	External context internal context
4.2	determine interested parties monitor and review information of int parties and requirements of interested parties monitor and review information of int parties and requirements		if interested party change in case requirements change	list requirements
4.3	determine boundary and applicability of the std. scope shall cover int and ext issue ,requirements of interested party and products and services shall apply all the requirements of the std. if applicable	scope of EOMS	if scope is revised	define scope define exclusion list of products andservices

	Scope shall be available as doc information shall state types of product and services and justification for exclusionall products and services given to learners shall be included			
4.4	shall establish, implement, maintain andcontinually improve QMS			process flow and
4.4.1	shall link to processes andthe interaction	list of process process interaction process details	processchanges	interactions
4.4.2	extent necessary shall have doc information for operationof processes doc information that processes are carried out as planned	processes manual /SOP/WI	Process operationchange	how process is carried out step by step approach

5. Leadership

5.1 Leadership and Commitment

General

Shall demonstrate leadership and commitment wrt QMS Taking accountability for the effectiveness of the QMS

- Ensuring that policy and objectives are established for QMS and are compatible with context and direction of the organization
- Why management or owner need to define policy and objective? Many companies work with only sales target not realizing that other process targets are equally important for overall growth of the company.
- Owner involvement is seen as a symbol of importance for the activity and also owner is a major share holder of the profit made by using working system effectively.
- Ensuring the integration of QMS requirements into the organization business process-this is needed because people need not get the impression that business is different from that of ISO system but should accept that ISO is part of business-related work.

- Promote use of process approach and risk based thinking—process approach help to define targets and also gives measurement against expected output.
- Ensuring that resources needed are available—this is required to have smooth functioning and also to know cost of resources and the returns gained.
- Communicating the importance of effective quality management and conforming to QMS requirements—people need to know the importance and the impact it can cause on the business. Ensuring that QMS achieves intended results—this is most important for any business through review of targets
- Engaging, directing and supporting person to contribute the effectiveness of QMS all staff and also external experts as per need have to know the direction and support expected.
- Promoting improvement to ensure encouragement of good performance.
- Supporting other management roles to demonstrate the leadership –this is needed to have better results from all the process owners on long term basis.

Customer focus

- Shall demonstrate leadership and commitment wrt customer focus Every business has to select who is your customer and knowingly or otherwise need to have policy keeping in mind the type of customers you intend to serve .
- Is it meaningful to focus customers and then form policy to serve them or take any customer only if they are as per your policy norms?
- Can college give admission to any student who pays them fee and maintain any reputation or std?? Selecting wrong customer or not establishing customer
- selection norm can seriously impact business .
- e.g. Hotel supplying idli and street vendor selling items on the cycle
- Customer and applicable statutory and regulatory requirements are determined, understood and consistently met—based on the type of customer the need to
- Understanding statutory and regulatory requirements is very important to continue the business on long term basis.

- Risk and opportunities which can affect conformity of product and services and ability to enhance customer satisfaction are determined and addressed – business risk for each type of product and services could be different and need to be reviewed for action purpose.
- Methods of measuring customer satisfaction need to be evolved and based on the feedback gathered one has to take timely decision and action to get benefitted from the same .

5.2 Policy

Establishing the Quality Policy

- Shall establish, implement and maintain a policy—this is needed to give direction to the working of all operations and communicating to the external world about your intent in implementation of the std. –Policy is way of life !!! and also the direction you intend to give to your business, why top management is expected take the trouble to form the same ?
- Answer is very logical and simple, if your policy is giving your business well defined direction and which will leads to deriving of process targets and objectives which in turn will get distributed in the process team in terms of the roles and responsibility and will get supported by the infrastructure and skilled manpower to perform effective operations, which are measured and evaluated against the set limits and are audited at defined intervals will result in something good in terms of profitability improvement and major shareholder of all this will be undoubtedly the management so their involvement plays a key role in the success of system implementation in efficient and effective ways.
- Shall be available and maintained as Documented information for review and for monitoring the effectiveness.
- One has to revisit the policy if desired results are not coming.
- Shall be communicated understood and applied within the organization—communication to all staff interested parties and eternal world is necessary so that they understand how their role is connected with the same and can apply their mind to know the impact of the system and process to the entire business.
- Shall be available to relevant interested parties—this is necessary to bring uniformity for review and for better understanding.

- Many times, it is found that interested parties in the business keep working in their own style creating their own methods of working which result in confusion and delays in working, to avoid this one has to know what the policy of the company towards quality of products and services is they intend to provide on a consistent level.
- Is policy made towards environmental factors, health and safety as well as for information security and energy management a part of business strategy? As all of them will impact the business in a great way .
- Many companies feel that they are not required to have policies for environment, health and information security not knowing how it can have positive or negative effects on the business.
- e.g. A motor manufacturing company in Africa found that productivity was improved by just providing exhaust fans in the production area as most of the workers were spending lot of time cleaning their sweating after every 10 min.due to hot and humid temperatures and used to take unwanted break for the same.
- One may be aware of the fact that many Japanese companies make it compulsory for all the staff to participate in the morning physical exercise before they actually start their routine working to ensure good health for the staff and that certainly has positive impact on productivity.
- Many pharma companies and food giants have great carc taken of the formulation of their key products as the success of their business entirely depends on the same, what will happen if Cadbury/Coca-- cola will lose the formulation to the competitors.
- Banking institute will never share passwords for the key data about the investors and other interested parties irrespective of actually taking the certification for information security as they know what can happen if information is available in wrong hands !!may throw them out of business.
- Each ISO std brings in value engineering if one has interest and inclination to understand and implement the same in their own business to the extent possible.
- Energy is one of the major cost Centre for many business as it is essential for office working as well as for machines and equipment to operate but very few companies know exact contribution of energy factor on the costing of their finished products /services and make conscious efforts to reduce them in a planned way.

- Food is a basic input we require to keep going and what can happen if your food safety does not meet basic requirements?
- One of the giant MNC software company in the world had to hold their operations due to non-availability of the software experts (40 numbers to be specific) at one major location as they suddenly suffer from loose motion and contingency plan for replacement of such lot was not thought of, reason --food safety violated by the canteen, thinking that it is not the main process of the software company, no one thought it should also have SOP until they suffered for the same.
- One can easily note from above discussion that for implementation of the ISO std. aiming for health, safety environment, food and information security and so on does not mean you need to be certified for the same but one has to have clear knowledge of the concept and how that can help your business and what is to be done for taking advantage from such information which will improve your business processes.

5.3 Organizational roles, responsibilities, and authorities

- Management Shall ensure that responsibility and authority for all roles are assigned, communicated and understood –this is necessary to monitor performance and also to avoid duplication of roles which not only cause confusion but also create ego issues for no good reason.
- Communication and understanding of roles and authority is key because Purchase head cannot release purchase order without account team support and acceptance that his decision for selection of supplier is final and is authorized to define the payment terms for the contract with the supplier which will be followed by his account team.
- Responsibility is duty assigned to the staff or contract team and authority is the decision making power associated with the same.
- Many times when people are appointed it is good practice to give them induction about their own section as well as other sections and make them understand how they are interlinked for delivering final product and services.
- Generally in most of the industries, responsibility is indicated but very few cover authority and accountability with the same as they can make or break the working system to a greater extent if not understood properly.
- Shall assign responsibility for conformity to QMS –this means cover all processes as per the organization chart covering entire business cycle from customer selection to delivery of service and product.

- What can happen if pilot and cabin crew exchange their roles or doctors and nurse have role changed during a surgery? Answer is simple and clear certain death for the customers, but if roles are not clearly understood and explained in any business it can give slow poisonous effect to the business so it is very crucial to confirm the same while the team is appointed and also when they are promoted during the working life.
- In case Harbhajan opens the batting and Sachin bats at no 11 both will surely do their role for batting but at the end team will lose for not giving them correct order, so it is also important that after giving role to all one must have correct sequence of operation as a part of SOP.
- Stores team, due to lack of clarity of roles start giving offers to customers and sales team start inspection work what will be the end result? Hope it is good enough example to note the effect one can have due to above clause for any business.
- Mind you it happens in many SME/MSME companies unknowingly which contributes to losses and downfall of business Process deliver intended output which is measurable and is aligned with the business goals of the company.
- Reporting on performance of QMS and opportunity for improvement is necessary for all processes and method as well as frequency of reporting need to be indicated to get better picture of company position.
- Reporting to cover minimum information about target set and achieved, area for improvement and decision taken by process head and details needed from management in terms of decision and resources is very effective for any business.
- Many times reporting happens only when there is serious issue or problem but not on regular basis as people do not like to get their working under a scanner even for improvement purpose!!! Ensuring promotion of customer focus throughout the organization-company is successful if customer requirements are understood by all process teams and they deliver as per the expectations of all customers.
- Map customer needs with all processes of the company.
- Integrity is maintained when changes are planned and implemented—changes may be planned if customer needs change get modified or cancelled and one has to evolve a process for ensuring smooth working during such changes.

Records related to clause 5

5.1

- Ensure establishment of policy and objective
- Ensure integration of QMS process and business process
- Give resources and engage, direct and support person for QMS
- Ensure QMS achieves results and promote improvement

5.2

- Define and display Quality policy
- Communicate the meaning and make it available to interested parties

5.3

- Define responsibility and authority of all roles and communicate
- Make reporting on performance of QMS
- Ensure promotion of customer focus
- Define change management

Case study-Indicate correct /wrong/may be possible case study -5.0

1. Management vision and mission is considered as policy.
2. Objectives are set only for key processes.
3. Objectives are communicated to process heads only.
4. Feedback on other beneficiary is not needed and only learner feedback is obtained
5. Risk and opportunity for each product is not defined.
6. Policy is signed by process head
7. Policy is displayed on web site and given to all staff and is available for external providers
8. Appointment letter indicate post but no responsibility and authority
9. Job description does not have authority indicated for all post

10 Contract staff role is given only in work order

Exercise -Roles, responsibility and authority

S. No.	Points to follow	Details
1	Roles for all staff	Indicate in appointment letter define job description ensure all are covered who are partof salary ensure there is no duplication of duty
2	Roles for contract staff	All the work done is measurable to the extent possible indicate the same in work order
3	Responsibility and linking of activities	Ensure the work is monitored and ismeasurable
4	Authority for all post	Indicate activity done by each process team distribute the activity for individuals
5	Linkage of objectives with roles and activities	Ensure no duplication
6	Reporting of targets	Ensure authority for work distribution and modification link authority for performance evaluation and iso work
7	Link of objective to process target	Define process objectives for all processes
8	Role for audit complianceand MRM	Define in MRM and audit
9	Performance evaluation methods	Review in MRM
10	Process improvements	Define and review in audit
11	Role for training and implementation	Define in HR process

6. Planning

6.1 Actions to address risk and opportunities

6.1.1

- Shall consider issues and requirements as per 4.1 and 4.2 to determine risk and opportunities QMS can achieve intended results
- Is it necessary to define risk for all processes? Can all risk be mitigated and opportunities created at once?
- Organization has many processes and out of which certain key processes are to be controlled like vital organs of the body and once risk is identified then classification should follow mathematical form to be able to have logical classification.

- Once the classification is done we need to decide which risks are critical and which one need to be avoided or reduced and also very important to live with acceptable risk to make life easy. e.g. how to identify and classify the risk of regular task done during working.
- Working on a computer is a simple activity-- is risk associated with this? What is critical in this level 1 type risk–simple one must not have virus during working as it is very essential to avoid this for proper working, which risk needs to be reduced –level -2 type of risk computer may not have storage capacity sufficient for data storage and can lose data due to same, this can be improved by additional RAM and then what is acceptable risk in this ?
- Very simple non-working of mouse or keyboard is acceptable—level 3 type of risk as replacement will not cost much and can be done easily.
- Enhance desirable effects—if we have good internet then data distribution will be faster and will support the operations in desirable way.
- Prevent, reduce, undesirable effects—as per the above example one has to understand each and every operation /task or activity for all processes so that critical risk can be prevented other risk can be reduced and some undesirable effects can be avoided.
- Achieving improvement—is possible if we can control all critical risk and keep reducing level —2 risk to acceptable limit.

6.2

- Shall plan actions to address risk and opportunities.
- Doing Business is risky as there are many things which can cause risk which are beyond our control and those which we can not because of lack of system knowledge.
- How to integrate actions in QMS processes—once we identify risk for all activities of a process it is important to know the impact of risk for one process for other.
- e.g Non procurement of material in time and of required qty.is a risk for purchase, will it have integrated effect on business –yes for sure.
- Material shortage will cause extra work for the production team to complete the batch qty. and also for the inspection team to do repeat inspection and store team for repeat material handling and shifting of the same to identified location.

- The effect and impact of the same will be based on the customer contract and importance of the material in the overall process.
- Evaluate effectiveness of actions—we need to know once the risk and opportunity table is established for each process it is very important to know actions taken are effective and are evaluated in time to get desired result. Each process need to have evaluation norms and action taken for improving the process need to be self-audited for improvement purpose. Without evaluation we do not know the effect of actions taken and that can be dangerous at times!!!

Quality objectives and actions to achieve them

Is objective necessary for business? Can we say we are doing good without any measurement for the same, philosophically it may sound nice but in practical world all the interested parties are always thinking of measurable results which they can justify to all stake holders and to achieve this result organization must keep on improving as a part of necessity without any choice as employees will not be happy to know there salary is increased without value attached for the same .

Failing to plan is worst, as one can fail in achieving the result you plan!!

Is target to be consistent with policy?

Should it be like sales should improve in good way!!

- Production to increase significantly?
- Quality should be good.
- Storage to be proper-
- Per employee profit has to be more etc.

6.2.1

- In any business however big or small there are some common factors for people to recognize the success of the business.
- Quantity may not mean quality but Quality needs to be measured in quantity and must keep improving consistently with more and more quantity to prove merit of product and service Supplied by the organization to customers across the globe.
- When we select employee at any post, we assure him/her a defined qty. of profit sharing in terms of salary or benefits but fail to evaluate the performance in same manner and end up in increasing the risk.

- In one of the interview in JAPAN, I was asked a simple question during my training in JAPAN, what is the similarity between electricity and quality in relation to any business? as am electrical engineer by profession, for a moment I was speechless by this kind of opening but then I said silently and firmly that both cannot be seen by naked eyes but can give shocks if not handled properly and my prof. replied with smile that you are here to learn exactly the same !!!
- Once we know that all objectives must be SMART– Specific, measurable, achievable, recordable, time bound.

  e.g. we need to increase sales of our product ABC/service XYZ to a value of 10 Cr .in this financial year is an example for the SMART target.
- Each process needs to have a SMART target and one must keep in mind that before targets are set one has to do gap analysis for understanding the present position and dream target to be achieved from the present situation using ISO principles.
- Many businesses unit do not want to display the targets set by the management in their mind but want their staff to achieve it for them and give them a pleasant surprise!!!
- Once you share and communicate to all teams about the target they need to make an action plan for the same to achieve it on factual basis.
- Action plan to cover resources, competency and training involved along-with steps for evaluation of the same.
- Can a scholar in school keep target of scoring 100% in each subject? One can but will have to be satisfied if you get 99.5% in the stipulated one year available with you, similarly each business need to keep their bandwidth for each target and also set those targets which will have quantum effect on the overall business.
- Can we reach moon by using bullock cart? No. even if you try for lifetime with best of your speed and ability, similarly resources and competency of each resource is key in defining the targets and also in achieving the same .
- Shall establish quality objectives at function level and processes needed for QMS –each target must have links to the roles team is expected to play and all the members are expected to relate the same for greater success.

- Each target has to be measurable as things which are not measured cannot be controlled and those we cannot control cannot be improved!!!
- When a cricket team is expected to win a match, role of batsman, all-rounder and baller as well as keeper and captain are supposed to get integrated and complementary to each other.

6.3

- Quality objectives Shall be Consistent with policy to have clarity in direction of the business path Measurable, take into account applicable requirement—what are applicable requirements?
- Can we have a product made in a factory which is illegal?
- Electricity is tapped from unauthorized sources to reduce costing of product? / Business need to be sustainable and this means need to follow the laws of the land to avoid unpleasant interruptions.
- Relevant to conformity of products and services and enhance customer satisfaction—for all business customer is the source of business and will remain focus point irrespective of the type of business.
- Now it is common to say that customer satisfaction need to be Monitored, communicated and updated, but it may not be possible to have 100% satisfaction for all customers and perhaps it may not be necessary as satisfaction comes at a price which is linked with company's performance and profits so one has to have golden mean between satisfaction and business sustainability.

Shall maintain documented information of quality objectives

- Shall determine what will be done in order to explain to investors and stake holders who will be investing in all possible resources, what resources will be required is to indicate manpower details to HR, machines and equipment data to purchase and production for procurement if not available, who will be responsible for guiding the team is important as they need to formulate a reporting system about monitoring the progress of the activity and plan or bar chart to be prepared to indicate when it will be completed, define time period and method of data presentation for understanding of how the results will be evaluated.

6.3.1

- Changes Shall be carried out in planned manner—It is possible that during the working life of any company people may change, equipment may get replaced, material and method of working can change which may result in change of target as well then it is important to communicate the same to the entire team involved In the working so that there are no losses due to lack of awareness of the changes.
- Shall consider purpose of changes and their potential consequences: it is necessary that changes are of two types one within the organization due to man, machine and material or method of working and other due to external factors such as statutory law modification like introduction of GST, change in electivity act etc. Both are going to be interrelated and change in one process target can have impact on the other like change in production capacity will have linkage with the target set for procurement of material and also will have relation with number of manpower required so it is important to review the target from the entire company level for obtaining better results.
- Shall Consider integrity of QMS: one has to review all the process targets as well as targets towards meeting legal compliance so that integrity is maintained.
- Shall Consider availability of resource which has capability to meet the requirements of the target, many times it is possible that internally competent team is not available then one can outsource the activity for desired level of accuracy and timely completion of activities .e.g. companies appoint CA, export agents and also many production process related work is given to approved suppliers for ensuring work completion in time. and allocation of responsibility and authority is given to internal as well as external service and material providers to have better understanding between the teams.

Records related to clause

6 6.1

- Risk and opportunity for all QMS processes
- Action plan and check effectiveness of the same

6.2

- Define Quality objectives
- Plan resources, responsibility and evaluation of results

6.3

- Define change management –purpose
- Indicate plan for changes in objective, documentation, roles and resources

Case Study –chapter 6 Case study -6.0

1. Risk and opportunities are defined only for key processes.
2. Action plan for each objective achievement is made but not evaluated
3. Objectives and risk of the process have no connection with each other.
4. Policy and objectives are linked and targets are derived from the same.
5. One of the objective is improve student results
6. Objectives do not link to legal compliance
7. Objectives are communicated by giving copy of the same as a part of Id card
8. There is no process for evaluation of objectives
9. Objectives will change if document is changed
10. Objectives will change if management team is changed

Exercise -to set objectives.

S. No.	Points to follow	Details	Who	How
1	Details needed/ information required toidentify process	Define inputs needed and output expected cover all activities done in the process understand present performance of the process study resources available and their capacity		
2	Activities in the process	Cover all activity and ensure they are distributed to team ensure that activity and outcome are linked		

3	Risk identification and classification	Identify all the negative impacts for last six moths for all processes once the risk is identified define the impact andprobability for each risk give marking for knowing the measurement of each risk based on the score classify the risk		
4	How to define opportunities	Define what can be improved for the process select the one which will have maximum impact give scoring for the selection each process target achievement to ensure objective achievement		
5	define measurable objectives	Select the process targets forall processes ensure they are measurable and can be evaluated define process for evaluation		
6	link policy and other requirements in objective setting	Ensure legal compliance for the organization review other requirements for linkage.		
7	link of objective to process target	Objective and process target to have links each process target achievement to ensure objective achievement		
8	establish strategic plan for achievement of objectives	Define target provide resources, team and allocate roles define review method for achievement select external experts if needed		
9	define change management system	Document changed management changed roles changed process changed, regulations and legal norms changed		
10	Process evaluation norms	Through review meeting through MIS reports thru internal audits		

ISO CLAUSE 6.0

clause ref.

6. Planning

6.1 Actions to address risks and opportunities

6.1.1

- Assurance that the QMS can achieve its intended outcome(s);
- Enhance desirable effects
- Prevent, mitigate or reduce, undesired effects;
- Achieve continual improvement

6.1.2

- Integrate and implement the actions into its QMS processes
- Evaluate the effectiveness of these actions

6.2 Organization's objectives and planning to achieve them

6.2.1

a Consistent with the educational organization's policy

b Be measurable

c Take into account applicable requirements

d Relevant to conformity of products and services and to the enhancement of learner and other beneficiary satisfaction;

e Continually monitored

f Communicated;

g Be updated as appropriate

6.2.2

- what will be done
- what resources will be required
- who will be responsible

- when it will be completed
- how the outcomes will be evaluated

6.3 Planning of Changes

- The purpose of the changes and their potential consequences
- The integrity of the educational management system
- The availability and readiness of internal resources.
- The allocation or reallocation of responsibilities and authorities
- The availability and readiness of external providers needed to implement. The change

7. Support

7.1 General

Resources

- Shall determine resources for establishment, implement, maintain and improve QMS—many times company management is clear about the benefits one can get through implementation of ISO std. In spirit, but to provide human experts for the same is not practically possible for SME/MSME business as they are running the business with minimum resources to make the business viable.
- While establishment stage one has to have experience of the ISO std., knowledge of business process and good communication skills – generally such qualities are available with either top management or key person of the company and sparing them for full time is impractical so it is better to appoint a team instead of single person for implementation of the system but it is very important that establishment is done by the best of the team so that even worst can follow the same, generally it is other way the one who is not so busy and can be spared without much difficulty is selected for establishment which results in documentation creation that only best can understand and others find it tough to follow.
- One has to note that maintenance post receipt of certification or post implementation is crucial as this involves identification of non-compliance and improvements and look for overall progress through systems.

- Shall consider capability and constraints on internal resources, when we draw a matrix of competency of staff wrt ISO implementation and maintenance we generally find that only few key members are aware of the importance and results one can get through system approach and mostly they cannot come out of their present roles as there is no replacement available and it can impact the process performance which cannot be accepted.
- In such a situation what needs to be obtained from external providers need to be defined during establishment, implementation and maintenance stage.
- Many companies appoint consultants as well as auditors from outside so that they can use their experience and can also involve part of company staff to have golden mean.

7.1.1 People

Shall determine and provide persons for effective implementation of QMS which can bring good results and operation and control of processes. It is important to know the purpose for which one is implementing ISO system

- For business entry /qualification of tenders
- To improve process performance and operation
- Have system working rather than person based approach
- Want to sale business to MNC customers/take over another business or plant
- Set up plants across the world with uniformity in working outputs
- To have edge over competitors.
- Based on the purpose one should select the team so that it is easy to match the requirements, however reason may differ but final aim is to have improved profitability and business expansion so it is necessary that competency for such team is well defined by management.
- One may find it tough to define exact requirements for the entire team of the organization when the business is just starting as choice is limited due to time constraint and budget limitation and one is not having any past records of the mistakes occurring in the operations, one can define time

- limit, budget and minimum acceptable competency for each post to get practical results but it is little easy for established business to keep it ready in terms of JD/Job description and have key performance indicators associated with the same.

7.1.2 Infrastructure

- Shall Provide infrastructure necessary for operation of process and to achieve conformity of product and services—while planning infrastructure following consideration can be thought of – Investment required
- Output expected Succession plan if required Life of the infrastructure
- Safety associated and efficiency This can include building, utilities, equipment, hardware, software, transportation, information and communication.
- In Japan there is a famous concept of Toyota line system which ensures that material flow is planned in such a way that there is no reverse and wrong directional flow of material this helps in saving time and energy in material handling and also make operations more effective and competitive, this also helps in conducting time motion study for all processes, but this can be thought of before building or buying the equipment and machines in a new place, for existing factory also one can realign the same to get better results, however for doing this business flow diagram need to be properly drawn before construction and start of working.
- Each process flow helps us in knowing the output expected and also life of each instrument and manufacturing or service related tools help in planning the finance accordingly as many times it is seen that due to sudden breakdown of key machines business suffer a lot and can impact their market reputation if they cannot control the replacement in time.
- One may not think of life expected of each infrastructure element while planning stage but it is very crucial to know the expected life and then to compare it with actual one to predict business operations and profitability in a better way.
- Hardware and software in today's world play a key role as most of the details of operations are recorded in software and for better data storage good hardware and servers are needed.
- Transportation is key factor in entire supply chain system, and it will be

impacting your business process depending upon the type of business one is having, however for selection of each infrastructure one can prepare a check list and verify the effectiveness o the same periodically to make modifications accordingly while planning a new plant location.

- It is observed that professional financial institutes conduct due diligence study for life cycle assessment to evaluate and predict return of investments and the same principle can be applied even when someone is investing their own funds from long term viability.

7.1.4 Environment for operation of processes

Shall determine, provide and maintain environment necessary for operation of process and to achieve conformity of product and services—this is applicable to all types of business, imagine what will happen if pharma and food companies find lot of dust entering the production area? Or chemicals and food items not stored as per the required conditions– what is the level of loss it can cause will depend upon the damages and nature of business, for any operation to be successful one must know the environmental factors associated with the same can you expect a surgeon to perform a surgery in open ground ?

- It can be fatal for the patient, in the same way working without knowing the environmental factors can cause wastage of items, reworking or even rejections at times.
- In simple terms even tea making process is highly dependent on temp. and without proper control it can spoil the taste.
- One also needs to define the parameters while planning the entire production cycle so the possible to plan measuring and monitoring devices accordingly.
- Environmental factors play a key role in production as well as preservation processes as many time it is seen that due to lack of preservation facility many factories have limitations on delivery and cannot even export the material where shelf life is tough to maintain.

7.1.5 Monitoring and Measuring Resources

General

Shall determine and provide resources needed to ensure valid and reliable results, for each process it is necessary to define control parameters and also to know the acceptable limit in which the process can give acceptable results.

- In medical line or hospitals one can not think of patient getting treated without measuring BP/Sugar, heart rate and pulse etc. what can happen if they are getting wrong results due to lack of effective measuring tools?
- It can cost your life or side effects for life time .
- Similarly not having knowledge of correct measuring device and the accuracy of results one will require for product conformity business will suffer endlessly in known or un-known ways.
- Both gold-smith and grocery business need their products to be weighed using weigh scale but can they both afford to have same accuracy in weighing?
- In similar way accuracy and selection of the equipment has to have proper study for ensuring that losses are reduced due to measurement issues.
- It is not expected to follow what other business is doing but important to know what your operations need for the desired level of accuracy.
- One of the factual case studies during my audit career will throw some light in this regard in practical terms and make you all realize the fact that every clause of the ISO std can get you profit if you wish to or it can take profit if you do not understand the application correctly.
- I was doing audit in one of the famous chemical companies where a simple question was asked to the senior inspector that do you have customer complaints in your area –he was in charge of filling section where perfumes were filled in the bottle and sent for packing section for delivery.
- He said with confidence and with lot of data that in last 30 years there was no customer complaint due to lack of qty. for which he and his team was mainly responsible, we asked him how they could achieve such a track record !!
- He was very confident and said let me show you how this is possible, so he demonstrated actual filling process by taking one of the glass bottles and filling it himself, after filling he asked me to consider you are the customer for the time being and see the level marked on the glass bottle and give your feedback !!you have paid for 10 gm of perfume, and I have given you something more to enjoy and weight was 11 gm, then he said you might think as an auditor I have given you more with a purpose to show my efficiency but you can check any bottle that is getting filled

and verify for yourself, I really tested his statement as a genuine auditor with few more samples to find that what he said was a fact.

- During my sampling company chairman also visited us to see how the audit is going and also to show his gesture and asked me if he could observe the audit process and when I said you are welcome he also witnessed the sampling and our method of verification, after the last sample was checked the inspector looked at me like a war hero and said now I hope you are convinced about our customer satisfaction and way of working, I said I feel sorry for your company!!
- He was taken by surprise and before he asked me why, I asked him how many bottles you dispatch every day?
- Now the chairman intervened and gave a figure of 10,000 per day, I said that means you are distributing 100 kg of perfume freely per day!!!
- Now inspector was really very upset and asked me what you are talking about ? I explained him that.
- 1 gm multiplied by 10,000 bottles is 100 kg and as examined you have consistently filled the bottle for one extra gm for today's delivery so am I right and if you are doing it for last several years I do not know how much amount of money your company has lost!!!
- Now chairman was very thoughtful and asked me sir my team has weigh scale and is calibrated having a certificate for the same, I said fine what is the accuracy of weigh scale it was +/- 1 gm and inspector told me that there were calibration accuracies up to .001 gm variation as well but cost of that accuracy of calibration was more by Rs. 2000 last 10 years back so I saved company's money by taking this accuracy class for calibration and I have certificate to prove the same.
- I asked him what the cost is of each 10 gm bottle, he said it is Rs.150 for the batch he is dealing with, then I said 100 kg will cost Rs. 1,50,000 per day extra do you feel you are right ?
- By this time chairman face changed drastically, he turned to me and said we should have done this audit even 2 years back I would have opened few more units in the money we wasted unknowingly following the wrong calibration accuracy of our weigh scale!!
- Friends, this can happen to anyone knowingly or otherwise but do we really think about it is a million dollar question, we have to ask our-self when we apply the std. to make profit for our business.
- What is the take way from the audit!!

- One must be sure of the measuring process applied for any operation in the company!!
- All the measuring process accuracy need to be reviewed considering the impact it can cause to the business!!
- One needs to evaluate the customer need and expectations and present level of satisfaction delivered and while it is certain for any business to keep their customer s happy, at what cost will the company exceed their satisfaction and for how long as well as for how many customers need to be reviewed by management otherwise stage will come that company will have nothing left to continue on long term basis.

e.g. All Passengers are railways customers but will railway allow the passenger who buys second class ticket to travel in AC first class and have same comforts ? And if they start doing it what will happen to those who pay for first A.C. fare to have additional comfort?

- Shall ensure that resources are suitable for specific type of monitoring and measurement activities and are maintained to ensure continued fitness for purpose.
- This can be best understood if you are in the hospital business where generally medical experts always think that they are above all procedures and are life saving god for all human being which is certainly true but what will happen if they get LAB records which are not accurate, their Blood Pressure machine gives wrong reading and equipment kept for measuring patient health parameters are not functioning as required ?
- With all the expertise they have, patient will have tough time to survive, similarly if batch formulation is wrong due to weigh scale not having proper accuracy, we can certainly reduce our population in a speedy way.
- Many times, people think that it is crucial for food and pharma and medicine business to have such arrangement but not having proper monitoring and measurement mechanism can ruin any business profitability and reputation in no time.
- I would give real life example to throw some light on the same.
- Few years after our college days, I met one of my friend accidently during my travel to karantaka for audit, he was a hotel owner and doing very well, after the greeting he asked me will your ISO be useful to my hotel operation where we deliver IDLI and Wada in fastest possible

time to our customers without having too much documentation like your ISO std. and most of my customers do not even no full form of ISO to get any market and sale benefit out of it(usually ISO documentation is considered as unwanted and is a topic of fun in most of the business owners), I told him I am not sure how much certification can add but implementation of some principles in spirit can add to your profits by all means if you wish to, as he is well qualified person immediately, he took his pad and said let me know in more depth how it can work for me.

- I asked him how much is the wastage in your business and how you define and understand the same? He laughed at this and said am not an industrialist to keep such data on records but to answer you it may be around 5%.
- I said can we do some measurement so that it is acceptable to both of us, he agreed for it and based on my request defined his term for wastage of food as the one which is rejected due to storage condition or shelf life issue and thrown and also one during the cooking process without considering the one wasted by the customers during eating as the same is paid for.
- He asked his account person to maintain records of each item thrown due to wrong storage because of excess inventory, poor conditions of storage, rats eating onions in the go-down etc. and came with a figure of 18 %, similarly he ordered his team to give the figure for loss in cooking, as there was no measurement of items issued Vs items used in cooking for each menu card products it was not easy until he physically set the process for few key items on sampling basis to know a figure of 8%.
- After the measurement was completed, he was looking sad, and he admitted candidly that what profit I considered is happening over the years is not what I really get as my calculations for wastage are having big difference in the estimated Vs real figures.
- For many businesses this example is a sad fact of life as they do not make a plan for accurate measurement of their operations to give desired results and start wondering why the profits are not seen in spite of good efforts put in by the entire team.
- After our meeting, I requested him to make a SOP for each item they serve on the menu card and also have material issue records for the same to know wastage in the cooking process and have stock records for all items they purchase for hotel food preparation and define inventory levels as per the consumption pattern based on the data of last few

months, find out how his food raw material can give him just in time delivery and then call me for audit after things are working as per plan.

- I forgot the incidence after getting into my routine work and after few months was surprised to receive my friend's call for audit invitation, after reaching his place, he said look I have only done what we discussed that is set inventory level, define location for each item in store, record all material issued and consumed during cooking and wastage at stores and no one in my team knows what is ISO and requested me not to ask anything of it, I said we will only check what you have done and is it useful?
- To our pleasant surprise with his conscious efforts and teaching to his team the levels were now 12 and 6 % instead of 18 and 8 %.
- His team said now we are able to have a more system driven approach and have reduced our working pressure about how much food is really available ?
- We can serve the customers in the time they expect and more importantly are able to generate more profit from the similar kind of turnover of the customers.
- They started realizing that by following few key steps and by maintaining records which they can take action on results in profitability which can be done by aby business without actually having a certificate part of it.

7.1.5.1

- Shall retain appropriate documented information as evidence of fitness for purpose of monitoring and measurement resources.
- We all have vehicles used every now and then for business and for individual use, why we maintain records for the fitness of the vehicle when we know that vehicle is fine every day we ride on it and indirectly test it as well, importance of having the validation of the vehicle done by authority is to ensure that what is tested by the service center is what is specified in the statutory regulation.
- This is simple as far as it is linked to vehicle but for every business one has to define what is the documented information one will require to assure himself about the fitness of his/her own business and so it is necessary to have such details reported on regular basis so that one can learn from them and take timely decision if required.

- Many times, company spend heavily due to lack of proper documentation in the day to day business.
- We know what the documented information are necessary for our personal life but still spend lot of time in searching them due to our inability to maintain them with proper system.
- Imagine what can happen to a person going for interview and not finding his degree certificate ?
- Can cost him the job opportunity, doctor not having blood group of patient who need to be operated on emergency basis –can cost life, businessman wanting to go abroad is not able to locate the passport and visa papers?
- Can cost business. Similarly, one must identify and define method of preservation of all those information which can have impact on the business.
- In Japan, for most of the companies document and information searching time has a target set– must be available in less than ''2'' minutes and it has a huge business value for those who can understand it.
- In case you see this point as a possible opportunity to speed up the operations just make your own study by finding out how much time your business needs for finding the correct documented information needed for your working and then see the effect it can cause on your operations.

7.1.5.2 Measurement Traceability

- Measurement equipment Shall be calibrated or verified at specific intervals prior to use against traceable std, basis used for calibration and verification shall be retained as documented information
- For each business, key operations are required to have the measurement done with equipment and instruments to ensure that the operation is carried out under controlled conditions and all the critical control parameters are measured to the desired level of accuracy.

e.g. in tea making operation, temp. for which one has to boil the tea mixture can impact the final taste so it is important to have control on the same and scientifically to maintain the consistency of control it is preferred to measure the same with a temp. indicator that can assure the operational consistency.

- It is very simple in above example but in business many times due to lack of knowledge of correct measuring parameter and equipment one can suffer for no good reason –imagine if your BP measuring machine is not calibrated and doctor will refer the wrong reading to give you treatment.

- One cannot blame him totally as instrument selection is a key factor and contribution to process results and their impact on final product or service.
- Measurement equipment Shall be identified in order to determine the status, safeguarded from damage which would invalidate the status and further measurement results.
- Once the process flow is defined for each process covering key control parameters for main operations then it is important to define status of performance of the measuring device at regular intervals and have defined method of proper maintenance of the same.
- One must understand how to read the calibration certificate correctly and be able to relate the same with the business operations which will have direct effect on the final product and service quality.
- Company Shall determine if validity of previous measurement is affected when equipment is found unfit for the purpose and shall take actions as necessary.
- This concept is simple to implement when it is related to the physical tools and equipment as they are usually checked before working and measurement results are easy to compare with those required for the purpose of declaration of fitness of equipment but with automation of process and use of software to issue material and also carry operations such as batch mixing and formulation etc it is very important that all such software are validated by expert and operation team is aware of the same to carry out the required checking at key intervals to prevent mistakes in the same as the material wrongly mixed in the batch may not be useful at all for the company and can cost loss of profits.
- Details of such validation need to be preserved for two things –to understand. The process and secondly to train the new person in the quickest possible time.

7.1.6 Organizational knowledge

- Company Shall determine knowledge necessary for the operation of its process and to achieve conformity of products and services-every company has certain way of working and methodology to follow to reach to final stage of products and services.

- Electrical Panels produced by Siemens and that of ABB are doing same functions but have different manufacturing processes followed and may also have different skill sets required from the work force to acquire as production equipment used, material quality and team capability differs from one company to another. This is also applicable in the business of food manufacturing, which is why the same product has different ways of manufacturing.
- A common point for all the business unit is that product conformity and service conformity as defined in the quality plan need to be achieved with minimum wastage, rework and rejection.
- In order to make it possible each company should define the process acceptance norms and also give knowledge of the same to the working team so that quality is monitored during the process stage and not at the end where rework and rejection will impact delivery and cost for the company.
- Knowledge shall be maintained and made available—it is most important to maintain the knowledge of working in terms of work instruction or standard operating procedure covering all the points of working so that even if the regular team is not available for whatever reason the work will not suffer for quality and quantity.
- Knowledge is the ability of individuals having the required skill to give desired results using the information made available to them in the quickest possible time.
- While addressing changing needs company shall consider its current knowledge and decide how to acquire additional knowledge—ISO has a nice std on knowledge management system ISO 30401 which describes how any business can turnaround the operations using knowledge management system.
- Knowledge is necessary to perform every operation and team involved in the same need to be aware of the same and also need to constantly think of improving the results by finding better way of working through additional knowledge.
- In any business every operation has a cost and time associated with it and unless you improve either of it improvements will not get linked to profitability.

e.g. In previous times people used Lathe machines to operate and produce various metal components in different parts of the world, after invention of

CNC machine, definition of working changed as the CNC machine works on set program and knowledge required to work on lathe machine may not have any significance for working on CNC machine which gives better productivity and in lesser time and cost if the volumes are more.

- As a part of automation of the plant, robots are replacing human element due to which knowledge of artificial intelligence is needed to operate such plants which is much different from managing a team of work force.
- For any business to be competitive usage of technology, innovation, latest trends need to be explored and acquired to the extent feasible and team need to be trained at the same pace to get the advantage of the same.

7.2 Competence

- Company Shall determine necessary competence for doing work which affect performance and effectiveness of QMS.
- Are all employees need to be competent? If you feel that their working can affect the company performance, then answer is yes and also if it is not having an impact then one has to redefine the business cycle and process flow because there is no point in creating a resource which has no role in company performance as it can reduce your costing.
- Competency is generally defined for post but in champion companies it is defined for each type of work carried out in the process because we may not have the same competency of people holding same designation.
- Business with clarity in competency find it easy to appoint people of the required skill, help them to acquire the one which is missing by giving training. and be in a better position to do performance analysis as the ref level is set for comparison purpose.

To explain this better would like to share experience I had in JAPAN.

- I was selected as the scholarship student, and we were given training on various subjects. /activities taking place in the factory.
- Our guide asked us a simple question–in your country how much is the training time and as students were from different parts of the world they replied from 6 months to one year.
- He was very surprised and said you have worked in which company in INDIA, I replied with proud feeling that in top engineering group of

company where we are called trainee for one year before being absorbed for the permanent post.

- In response to this, he said I have heard that your company is very good in many fields and they select meritorious candidates for job, I felt very happy to note that but he continued and said why a company of such class needs one year to explain what is expected from a new person?
- Is the process not set properly or the trainers not so skilled or the candidates have less capability to pick up required skill or details?
- He continued and remarked that training cost time, money and efforts and company has to be effective using all the elementsif they need to be world class.
- Our next point was how much is the average period in JAPAN, he said max.one month due to the complexity of job.
- We said how it is possible to know the required skill in such a short time –he did not react but promised us that he will prove his point practically which is the way of life in JAPAN Industries.
- We had a study tour of one famous company and my guide said can you do the assembly of a component without knowing what is the product, our reaction was very simple how it is possible?
- He took us to the factory head and requested him to release the material needed for assembly of electronic unit and told him that his team can give us the details in next one hour in English and share the SOP for doing the same.
- We though he is going crazy or perhaps want to prove us wrong, once we receive the SOP it was in video form with English titles and speech of what one should do for each step of assembly, we followed the same and could produce the component which was tested ok to our great delight.
- We wanted to know what the instruction is given to the regular work force so that they produce defect free items and found that everyone had a different set of instruction with few having video and few having statements in the Japanese language.
- Our guide was looking at us and the shock we had by understanding that same work completion is done in different styles of instructions and yet it is defect free. before we ask he explained the concept in a very different way!!

- For each operation of the company they distributed the manpower in three types –one called as expert who can train others for doing the operation, second –who can work under guidance of expert and third has no skills and knowledge and is a trainee.
- Instruction for expert was very short indicating key control parameters and care to be taken and maintain the same while working, second category of team had statements with a sequence of operation and explanation of what will happen if they do not follow the same in proper terms, third set –people like us who had no knowledge and skill about the working had everything in video where like a child the picture explained everything with a title in English and was followed by very detailed approach which any one can follow.
- When we all asked why they have to do all this different type of SOP preparation for each and every operation they have in the factory—he without showing any expression said we do not have the liberty of having experts for all the work all the time and we want it to be defect free all the time!!
- We just validated our video SOP successfully when your assembly was tested ok, to our further notice all the SOP were drafted by people from outside experts and audited from another panel not from the company.
- Factory head explained that people are not having time to think moment they enter the unit as they have to achieve tough targets every day in limited time and with no or zero defects so we always get the expert for the job and achieve our targets by just following what is given by the expert, sometimes it is possible that few of the team members do not understand the same then we use our training panel to ensure that they follow the same and for every operation time required to complete the work is indicated for each level of person that is for expert, one who can work with guidance and totally new person and time is also set for one category person to move to next so that efficiency is increased and in case of emergency, we can shift our manpower accordingly as we know who are having what kind of capability in proven way.
- Company Shall ensure persons are competent on basis of education, training or experience applicable take actions to acquire competence, retain documented information as evidence of competence—In every company management has certain idea about what should be the education to perform certain task and also experience associated so that the work is performed as per expected level.

- Many times, it is not feasible to get ideal combination described in the concept stage and hence one has to move ahead with whatever manpower available
- As one cannot wait for perfect combination to be available and also willing to join and work with the company on long term basis.
- Right person for right job!! is good to have but it is practical to see that training is given in such a way that any person is able to perform right job all the time, this may also cover establishment of SOP and work instruction on the basis of the famous Japanese concept – POKAYOKE –(Mistake proofing) of the activity and process work, this not only allows you to save on the budget as one can hire lower qualified person and still make them work using effective training and documentation tools and if the documented information is retained as indicated in previous example one will have flexibility to classify the instruction as pert he education and experience variation without affecting quality of finished product and service.
- Lot many successful companies in the world have clear classification of category of work force and is linked to all possible tasks to be performed for work completion.
- Training is made in such a way that conversion of knowledge and skill to actual performance is done in the shortest possible time.
- Companies can adopt time line for conversion of un-skill staff to semi –skill and semi –skill to skill level and monitor the output at regular intervals, it is very common to note that success of the company operation will heavily depend upon the speed of conversion of the skill set to actual performance. In Japan many top grade industries keep giving constant training to the staff so that improvements are visible in short span of time.
- Common topics selected for the same are linked to work related skill improvements, health, disaster management, multiskilling in various areas so that they can work as succession support if required.
- Generally, world class companies look for following points as a part of competency because they believe in long term association with the staff –again in Japan people are associated with the company for generations having very strong bonding with each aspect of the working and management.

- Some of the points which are used for competency mapping are – Education, skills, experience, health, legal records and previous history or background in the career of the candidate.
- Person with color blindness cannot operate crane or vehicle as it can lead to disaster, same way someone with lot of health issues cannot work as loader for a long time.
- For each post skills required can have different impact –e.g. good communication skills will directly impact sales and market based activity but may not have so much effect if not available with someone working in packing department working as per the guidelines, similarly knowledge of handling people is necessary for production supervisor but not so much for account team who will be entering data in tally day in and day out, so ideally it is recommended to have excel sheet made with markings given for each skill and also time required to establish the same if the same is missing in any work force. Company, who is performance, driven will have gap analysis done for competency required and available and the training plan to fill the same will be prepared so that work will not suffer due to lack of skills at certain position.
- Competency also covers all those who are involved in training –internal and external experts as one cannot expect Israel commando to train security person, one should also not bring a layman for the same as each function has its own importance in the working of the company which need to be respected with due regards.
- Capable person for each job in right time can impact company performance in Significant ways
- Competency is a serious topic when it comes to individual health, education etc. as no one will approach a doctor because they are cheap or take admission for our kids to a school just on fee as criteria, but it requires same approach in industrial work if we need to have our business sustainable.
- Most of the times we find people do job not as per their liking but out of compulsion and family requirements and so lot of them are not happy in what they do on regular basis and not able to work in the field of liking can de- motivate team on long term basis but it is impossible to also have people having good competency in the field of their choice, so alternative would be to look for skill set utilization and create awareness of the same to the management in best possible way, today we pay people for what they are expected to do as per defined set of roles but if HR/

Management improve their awareness of all the hidden talent in the staff they can think of modifying the roles given to staff and get better results.

- Capable leader can bring best out of his team and on the other hand can promote worst in the team unknowingly, so competency of leaders and management plays a key role in the progress of the company, people always say company management is good or bad they never say company infrastructure or material is bad but finally all human resource is leaving the boss of the company in practical terms.

7.3 Awareness

- Company Shall ensure that persons are aware of Quality policy, objectives, contribution to effectiveness of QMS including benefits of improved performance and implications of non- performance of QMS—
- Let us assume expert medical professional team highly competent in their area of work is going to operate on a patient they do not have any historical data available or in simple terms are not aware of the allergy, side effects one can have or serious illness history then what will be the result –based on the destiny patient may or may not survive, in individual case the result is fast but in business terms the result can take time and be like slow poison –imagine you have hired highly competent retired ambulance driver for delivery of goods and they are glass products, if the awareness is not given to the driver about the precautions to be taken while driving you will end up in loss of material and reputation .
- Material handling equipment operator is not aware of speed limits –can cause life, infrastructure, and damage to material due to rash driving and negligent working.
- Awareness is generally given in the form of training, notification, signages and also through verbal instructions depending upon the impact it can have on your working.
- Induction training is used to spread awareness about safety in working, disaster management and work permits as applicable to be obtained for safe working. Formal training is given where specific skills are to be improved in a defined interval.

Every business can have one of the two ways adopted for creating awareness

Learn while you make mistakes or learn not to make mistakes.

Choice of selecting the option is entirely with management, first option is easy as requires no efforts on training but can cause loss of material, equipment and also reputation, while second option will require efforts and time to be spent to avoid having any loss.

7.4 Communication

- Company Shall determine the internal and external communication relevant to QMS on what to communicate, when to communicate, with whom to communicate how to communicate and who communicates.
- Internal communication is of two types –one within each process or section that is sales team within themselves and other with other sections that is sales handing over job requirements received from customer to operations.
- In first case one has to be clear about what is method of communication for all the process activities within the process that is for sales or business development – how to record enquiry, what is the pattern for offer or quotation submission for business opportunity other than tender business, job handing over to operation, handling of complaints and feedback business promotion meetings etc., now one may think that why I must have forms and other documents for this as this is company matter in a way?
- Imagine if everyone starts sending offer in different ways considering his/her own pattern which may or may not contain all the required information which need to be communicated to perform the work in a desired way –it can only result in rework or rejection, it is necessary that all the team doing specific task have certain method adopted to ensure consistency of working and many times this is realized after having loss in business opportunity or in operations.
- In many MNC companies induction training module is prepared for effective orientation of the new member in such a way that they are aware of the task to be performed, method in which it is expected and educated for data or information storage after the task is completed this helps to reduce unwanted communication and also reduces time and efforts lost in providing such details again and again.
- Do you think by having this communication in a structured way one can save time and efforts then create your own ways to see that you spare less energy in explaining the internal team about the information necessary for work completion.
- Many times, it is seen that due to lack or wrong communication between

two process team delivery of service or material is affected and can cause loss to the company.

- How do you measure effectiveness of communication?

Here again I would share my experience in JAPAN .

I was there on a scholarship and on the very first day, I was introduced to all the team and also was given the induction training video for reference covering most of the work-related details in real depth.

- From next day I started working accordingly and was very surprised to note that no one communicated anything or rather had even a word with me except during lunch time and after office hours while leaving home, Initially I thought that because am non-Japanese they might be keeping a very reserve approach towards me as well as to other foreign work force.
- After 5 days I could not stop my self-requesting the manager for a 5 min. discussion and with great surprise on his face he called me to his cabin and asked me that what is the problem faced?

I replied that no one is talking to me about my work and am not clear what I am doing is correct or not. He took a pause and said can I ask you few things, and started asking me following points –

- Are you having clarity of what to do or what is your role –I said yes
- Do you have resources in terms of equipment /PC/Material and method of working given to you in writing—I said yes
- Are you clear about the same – I said yes
- Do you know how to report your working and are you doing the same as per the instruction given –I said yes
- Are people who are expected to report you doing it as per the norms –I said yes
- Are you finding any process rejections –I said no
- Do you know about all the facilities given by the company –like transport /canteen/tea machine and other facility like library and how to use them– I had no choice but to say yes.
- Lastly, he said are you feeling ok—Medically any problems faced –I said no am perfectly fine!!

He smiled and said did anyone informed you that you are making any mistake? I said that also someone need to speak to me and no one said anything till now.

- Finally, he asked me did you observe Japanese team talking to each-other during working time? I said no although I was not fully conversant with Japanese language, I was able to understand the same as part of our training so I replied to no.
- He went further and shared something very important for any business to follow –
- If you have clarity about working, you are having all the resources necessary to work made available and method of working and reporting known to you and also having the reporting made as per the system from your juniors then why people should speak with each other and reduce the production for no good reason!!!
- Unless they have problem with machines or material or there is medical issue or emergency situation they will not waste their time. Something I saw rarely that there was sound of only machines and equipment and people use to work exactly as per the norms to get maximum output for the company and nation.
- In such location one can see that they have taken lot of efforts to have a communication system established in such a way that people are able to deliver beyond expectations as there is no searching time for tools, equipment and spare parts, material required for production (they follow 5 ''S'' for the same), forms needed to indicate work done and each person used to take only 5-10 min. to prepare himself/herself for the day's work as per the target given by the manager .
- Business in today's time need to think about his concept and calculate the loss time only in searching material, manpower, instruction /decision given daily and efforts spent to measure the output.
- One can understand the importance of these systematic communication and impact it can have on productivity and profitability if we reduce the time in all non-productive activities with focus efforts.
- I am well aware that it is very tough to achieve such condition but one needs to apply our mind so that we can certainly improve our performance to some level.
- External communication is about dealing with external govt. agency for obtaining permissions and license to operate as well as to comply with the regulations and laws of the land.

- External communication is for three main activities—one for statutory compliance, second for dealing with customers and third for dealing with suppliers providing service and material.
- All the three stake holders are very important from business sustainability and hence communication with each of them need to be handled with care and with system.
- Skills and competency required to handle all of them is very different but one thing is common and that is all can largely impact your work.

One can define a chart for each of the three types of communication by considering following example as many time sit is seen that work is affected due to delay in obtaining compliance or renewal of the regulatory norms at work site even though funding is available.

- Companies lose money and reputation due to inefficient working from their material and service providers due to lack of proper communication in time, now big companies adopt software system like ERP /SAP to ensure that this is taken care irrespective of change in manpower however if one can use simple forms structure In sales and purchase process and follow them religiously similar results can be obtained even by SME /MSME range of companies.
- Ref communication chart attached for ref and guidance of how one can formulate a simple method of making every team member understand the system without much explanation.

7.5 Documented information

7.5.1 General

- Company QMS Shall include documented information required by this std. Documented information determined by the organization necessary for effectiveness of QMS.
- Every Business has some kind of documents followed at some point by few team members while the work is being carried out in all locations.
- Why do we need documented information for effectiveness of the QMS or any other ISO system?
- Let us understand it from a very different point, all the religions have their knowledge taken from written script in the form of Bhagwadgeeta, Kuran, Bible and many other religious books followed by many in the world for generations to have better living system.

- Now what will happen to any business if there are no contractual documents, no instructions followed in writing while clearing the goods from the system, no laws written for any country? One cannot imagine the interruption it can cause for the running of any business, today with lot of written scripts one finds it tough to get govt approvals without it perhaps no business will survive for long.
- Documentation requirements are given in every ISO std. because it has immense importance and can have a huge impact on the operational efficiency of all processes.
- Many of you must have heard the story about loss of information and it's effect due to diverse ability of individuals to pass the same to others in effective ways.

7.5.2. Creating and Updating

- Company Shall ensure appropriate identification and description, format, review and approval of suitability and adequacy.
- We start identification of name from birth till death for all human being.
- We have tickets issued during our bus/railway and flight reservations proper traceability to avoid inconvenience to all those who travel, similarly in business when you have created the system for convenience in working of those who work with you it is necessary to have proper numbering /title to all the information to be part of system.
- One must also note that what is adequate for certain level of competency of people may not have much relevance to those who do not have such competency, one must be clear at what point the suitability and adequacy need to be monitored for necessary action, as one can see all the clauses of ISO std are interlinked with each other one must be able to derive correct meaning out of it to ensure performance improvements.
- What is adequate for one business may not work for other as there are many control factors which govern the suitability of documentation and it's implementation.
- This is again very relevant when it comes to medical line –what will happen if you are treated by the doctors of any hospital for someone else medical records file as ref by mistake –your survival can be under threat!!
- What if farmer selects wrong soil for his crop, entire efforts will go in vain, if you get marksheet entered against your name by mistake –can cost you admission and career!!

- In business each piece of information has a significant impact on the process performance which in turn will affect quality of finished goods and services.
- Can any site/project afford to construct even part of the industrial plant with wrong or non-approved drawing and then must scrap it because it was not as per the latest approved information from the client?

7.5.1 Control of documented information

- Company Shall control documented information to ensure it is available and suitable for use when needed and it is adequately protected.
- This can be explained by one of my real time experience .
- In one of the ISO consulting assignment there was tender system followed and during closing meeting job was awarded to the lowest bidder –not to take any names because we need to understand the concept of the clause and not names, after the meeting we asked the winner that how he is able to afford less than 50% cost as compared to other companies who were all good to provide the services. The person just smiled and replied you are thinking of making profit from one company and am looking to cover his competitors as well in the process!!! Once I have data available.
- Now every company must have certain classification of the data and information available for working so as to protect the same
- Previously companies used to keep the accounting files –hard copy in lock conditions and even today people use passwords for logging and have many software who will monitor your PC for the details you work on during the day and also will have provision for not opening the individual mails or other sites through Google.
- Details of software validations are retained as proof of data security and information security audits are conducted to ensure business information marked as critical is protected.
- Company Shall address following activities –distribution, access, retrieval and use storage and preservation including legibility control of changes, retention and disposition.
- Every documented information established for work related operation need to be distributed as per roles, access must be given keeping in mind information security, retrieval need to be in less than 5 min. as an example because searching the information available and in use is

most frustrating experience and generally amounts to 2 to 3 man-hours every day for many industries, one can define document and information searching time as one of the key objectives so every effort will be made as a part of action plan to see that all documented information is stored properly and preservation norms are modified as per the volume of data and need for usage.

- This has great significance to field like education and medicine where if the system is adopted in spirit you will have less chance of student getting wrong question paper, having delayed start due to lack of availability of question paper or paper having questions beyond syllabus, delay in declaration of results and people caught in copy etc.
- In medical line one can face delay in treatment due to lack of proper documentation, wrong treatment given due to lack of knowledge of patient history, medicine not in useful condition due to storage and preservation point etc.
- Company Shall identify documented information from external origin necessary for operation of QMS—This is needed for basic logic that customer requirements or statutory details for any company is the reason of existence for almost all companies and need to have unique identification for storage and retrieval.
- Documented information retained as evidence Shall be protected from unintended alteration Once the information is available then basic logic is it must be followed for all purpose and protected because any modification made can impact the business in a big way.

Records related to clause

7 7.1.

- Define list of resources needed for all processes.
- Compare adequacy and define list of external providers for products, services and for process
- Define list of manpower available for process
- Make a list of infrastructure available and environmental factors linked to process.
- Define monitoring and measuring resources for process.
- Retain fitness for purpose for all such resources.

- Make calibration plan and retain records of calibration.
- Identify fitness status for all equipment and define process for disposal of out of form equipment and review of records taken with such equipment
- Define organizational knowledge for operation of each process, make plan. to acquire additional knowledge-link to induction training

7.2

- Define competence needed for each post linked to all processes in terms of education, training, and experience.
- Compare the same with available resources of each process.
- Retain documented evidence for the same.

7.3

- Define awareness plan for policy, objectives, and contribution to QMS.
- Awareness for the benefits of performance and consequences of non-conformance

7.4

- Define internal communication plan and define all details.
- Make external communication plan and indicate full details.

7.5

- Define master list of all documents for all processes.
- Make identification, review, and approval plan for all documents.
- Define distribution, access, retrieval, use, protection, storage and preservation, retention, and disposition norms for all records.
- Make list of documents for external origin and apply protection and preservation norms for the same.

8. Operation

8.1 Operational planning and control

- Company Shall plan, implement and control the process needed to meet requirements for products and services and to implement actions
- Determine requirements for products and services.

- Establish criteria for process and acceptance of products and services determine. Resources needed for achieving conformity of product and services.
- Define resources needed for achieving conformity.
- Indicate process implementing control.
- Determine, maintain, and retain documented information that process is carried out as planned.
- Demonstrate conformity of products and services
- Output of planning shall be suitable for operations.
- Shall control planned changes and review consequences of unintended changes take action to mitigate adverse effects Shall control outsourced process.

8.2 Requirements for products and services

8.2.1 Customer communication

Company Shall provide information about products and services, handling enquiry, contract and changes, obtaining customer feedback relating to products including complaints, handling customer property, establish requirement for contingency action

8.2.2 Determining the requirements for products and services

Company Shall ensure that product and service requirements are defined, applicable statutory and regulatory requirements necessary by the company Company Shall meet the claims for products and services.

8.8.3 Review of the requirements for products and services

Company Shall ensure ability to meet product requirements offered conduct. review before committing to supply.

8.2.3.1

Company Shall review specified requirements by customer, delivery, and post. delivery activity

Not stated but intended for use, statutory and regulatory requirements applicable, requirements different to those specified.

Company Shall ensure all requirements differing from previous one is. resolved

Company Shall confirm requirements before acceptance when customer does. not give documented statement

8.2.3.2

Company Shall retain documented information on the results of the review, on new requirements of products and services

8.2.4

Changes to requirements for products and services

Company Shall that relevant documented information is amended and relevant persons are made aware of the changed requirements

8.3 Design and Development of Products and Services

8.3.1 General

Company Shall establish, implement, and maintain design and development process to ensure provision of products and services.

8.3.2 Design and development planning

Company Shall consider nature, duration and complexity of the activities required stages including reviews, required verification and validation activity responsibility and authority involved in the process internal and external resource needs, control interface between persons involved need for involvement of customers and users, requirements for subsequent provision of products level of control expected, documented information to demonstrate design and development requirements are met

8.3.3 Design and development inputs

- Company Shall determine the requirements.
- Company Shall consider functional and performance requirements information derived from previous designs, statutory and regulatory requirement, codes and ref std. consequence of failure due to nature of product.
- Input Shall be adequate, complete, conflicting inputs shall be resolved. Shall retain documented information of the inputs.

8.3.4 Design and development controls

Company Shall define results to be achieved.

Company Shall conduct review to evaluate ability to meet requirements, verification activity to ensure outputs meet the input requirements, validation to ensure products and services meet the requirements, controls for actions taken on problems determined during review, verification and validation activity.

Shall retain documented information about all the controls.

8.3.5 Design and development outputs

- Company Shall meet the input requirements.
- Company Shall are adequate for the process for provision of products and services, include ref monitoring and measuring requirements and acceptance criteria, specify characteristic essential for intended purpose and safe and proper provision Shall retain documented information of the outputs

8.3.6 Design and development Changes

- Company Shall identify, review and control changes so that there is no adverse impact on conformity of products and services
- Shall retain documented information on design and development changes, results of review, the authorization of changes, action taken to prevent adverse impact.

8.4 Control of Externally Provided Processes, Products and Services

1.1.1 General

Company Shall ensure that external process, products, and services conform to the requirements

- Company Shall determine the controls to be applied for the same controls Shall be for Products and services intended for incorporation of company's product and services
- Products and services provided directly to the customers on behalf of company Process provided as a part of decision of the company.
- Company Shall determine and apply criteria for evaluation, selection, monitoring of performance and re-evaluation of external providers based on ability to meet requirements Company shall maintain documented information of these activities and actions arising from evaluations.

Type and extent of control

- Company Shall ensure that external process, products, and services do not adversely affect company's ability to deliver consistent products and service s to the customer.
- Company Shall ensure that external process, products, and services remain within the control of QMS determine the controls to be applied for the same controls Shall define the controls to be applied to external provider and resulting outputs.
- Company Shall take into consideration potential impact on the of external providers on ability to consistently meet customer and regulatory requirements and effectiveness of the controls applied by the external providers, determine the verification to ensure external providers meet requirements.

8.4.3 Information from the external providers

- Company Shall ensure adequacy of requirements prior to communication with external providers.
- Company Shall communicate external providers about process, product and services to be provided.
- Approval of products and services, method, process and equipment and release of product and services, competence and qualification of persons, interaction with the comnpany,control and monitoring of performance, verification and validation of company and customer inspection at the external provider's premises.

8.5 Products and Service Provision

8.5.1 Control of Products and Service provision

Company Shall implement production and service provision under controlled conditions which shall include.

Availability of documented information that define.

- Characteristics of products to be produced and services to be provided or activities to be performed.
- Results to be achieved.
- Availability of monitoring and measuring resources

- The implementation of monitoring and measuring activities at appropriate stages to verify criteria for controls meet the acceptance norm of product and services.
- Use of suitable infrastructure and environment for operation of process
- Appointment of competent staff, Validation, and periodic re-validation of ability to achieve planned results of the processes where outputs cannot be verified by monitoring and measurements.
- Competent persons with required qualification
- Implementation of actions to prevent human error.
- Implementation of release, delivery and post-delivery activities

8.5.2 Identification and Traceability

- Company Shall use suitable means to identify outputs when necessary to ensure conformity of products and services Company Shall identify status of outputs wrt monitoring and measurement requirements throughout the production and service provision.
- Company Shall control the unique identification of the outputs when traceability is a requirement and Shall retain Documented information necessary to enable traceability.

8.5.3 Property belonging to customers and external providers

- Company Shall exercise care when it is under company's control or being used.by the company
- Company Shall identify, verify, protect, and safeguard customer property. Provided for use in products and services.
- When property is lost, damaged, or found unsuitable for use Company Shall report this to customer and external provider and Shall retain Documented information on what has occurred.

8.5.4 Preservation

- Company Shall preserve the outputs during production and service provision to the extent necessary to ensure conformity of products and services.

8.5.5 Post delivery activities

- Company Shall consider statutory and regulatory requirements potential undesired consequences associated with products and service, nature, use and intended life time of its products and services, customer requirements and feedback

8.5.6 Control of changes

- Company shall review and control changes to ensure continuing conformity of products and services with requirements.
- Company shall retain documented information describing the results of reviews and changes and action arising from the review.

8.6 Release of products and services

- Company shall implement planned arrangement s at stages to verify that product and service requirements are met.
- Company shall not proceed for release to customer unless planned arrangements are completed or approved by relevant authority or customer.
- Company shall retain documented information on the release of products and services which shall include. Evidence of conformity with acceptance criteria, traceability of persons authorizing release

8.7 Control of non-conforming outputs

Company Shall ensure outputs that do not conform to requirements are identified and controlled to prevent unintended use or delivery.

8.7.1

- Company Shall take action based on the nature of non-conformity this shall apply to products after delivery or during or after provision of services
- Company Shall deal with outputs in following ways— Correction, segregation, containment, or suspension of provision, informing the customer obtaining authorization for acceptance under concession.
- Company Shall verify conformity when NC outputs are corrected

8.7.2

Company Shall retain documented information on describing the non-conformity, action taken, concessions obtained authority deciding the action in respect of Non-conformity

Records related to clause 8

8.1.

- Define requirements for products and services.
- Establish acceptance criteria for products and services.
- Define resources and make planning to get intended output.
- List outsourced processes and their control
- Establish change management for the process.

8.2

- Define customer communication chart covering enquiry, order review, feedback, property, complaints and contingency actions
- List statutory and regulatory requirements for products and services
- Maintain documented information about contract review and amendments and changes to products and services

8.3

- Define design and development process
- Establish design and development plan covering activity like, stages of review, verification and validation authority involved in the process internal and external resource needs, control interface between persons involved and customer interface
- Documented information for plan to be kept
- Shall retain documented information of the inputs
- Shall retain documented information of all the controls.
- Shall retain documented information of the outputs
- Shall retain documented information on design and development changes, results of review, the authorization of changes, action taken to prevent adverse impact.

8.4

- Define external providers for products and services which are to be incorporated in company's products and services

- List external providers who will give service and products directly to customer on behalf of the company
- Determine and apply criteria for evaluation, selection, monitoring of performance and re-evaluation of external providers based on ability
- Documented information of these activities and actions arising from evaluations
- Review impact of external providers on the products and services to be given to customer and on statutory compliance

8.4

1. Approval of products and services, method, process and equipment and release of product and services,
2. Competence and qualification of persons, interaction with the company, control and monitoring of performance, verification and validation of company and
3. Customer inspection at the external provider's premises for process where output is not directly measurable and for all other requirements of products and services

8.5

- Availability of documented information that define

  Characteristics of products to be produced and services to be provided as 8.5.1
- Retain Documented information necessary to enable traceability.
- Retain Documented information about customer property and external provider property and controls used to preserve.
- Define preservation norms for products and services.
- Establish post-delivery norms and review the impact of the same through intended life and feedback from customer.
- Retain documented information describing the results of reviews and changes and action arising from the review related to products and services.

8.6

- Retain documented information on the release of products and services which shall include Evidence of conformity with acceptance criteria, traceability of persons authorizing release –release note.

8.7

- Define non-conforming outputs till delivery and post-delivery and decide actions to be taken and record the same.
- Documented information on action of NCP or services.

9. Performance Evaluation

9.1 Monitoring, Measurement, Analysis and Evaluation

9.1.1 General

- Company shall determine what needs to be monitored and measured methods, analysis and evaluation needed to ensure valid results, when the monitoring and measurement shall be performed, when the results shall be analyzed and evaluated Company Shall evaluate the performance of the effectiveness of the QMS.
- Company shall retain documented information as evidence of the results.

9.1.2 Customer satisfaction

Company shall monitor customer perception of needs and expectations.

- Company shall determine the methods for obtaining monitoring and reviewing the information.

9.1.3 Analysis and Evaluation

- Company shall analyze and evaluate data and information arising from monitoring and measurement.
- Result of analysis shall be used to evaluate conformity of products and services degree of customer satisfaction, performance and effectiveness of QMS and planning implementation action taken to address risk and opportunities
- Performance of external providers, need for improvements to QMS.

9.2 Internal Audit

9.2.1

Company shall conduct internal audits at planned intervals to provide information on QMS, Company's requirements to QMS and to the international std. and QMS is effectively implemented and maintained

9.2.2

Company shall plan, establish, implement and maintain audit program, methods responsibility and reporting shall take into consideration importance of process and changes affecting the company and results of previous audits.

9.2.3

Company shall define audit criteria and scope select auditors and conduct. audits to ensure objectivity and impartiality.

Company shall ensure of audit are reported to management Shall take correction and corrective action without any delay Shall retain documented information as evidence of implementation of audit program and audit results

9.3 Management review

9.3.1. General

Company shall review company's QMS at planned intervals to ensure continuing suitability, adequacy effectiveness and alignment of the strategic direction of the company

9.3.2. Management review inputs

Company shall planned and carried out taking into consideration--Status of actions from previous review changes in internal and external issues relevant to QMS Information on performance and effectiveness of QMS Customer satisfaction and feedback from interested parties Achievement of quality objectives.

Process performance and conformity of products and services monitoring and measurements and audit results, performance of external providers, adequacy of resources, effectiveness of actions for risk and opportunities and opportunity for improvement

9.3.3 *Management review outputs*

Output Shall include decisions and actions related to

Opportunity for improvement Any need for change to QMS Resource needs

The company shall retain documented information as evidence of the results of the management review.

Records related to clause 9

9.1

Measure and analyze performance of QMS, Customer feedback, external. providers and retain documented information.

9.2

Define audit process and retain documented information as evidence of implementation of audit program and audit results

9.3

Define method to conduct management review and retain documented. information about review outputs

10. Improvement

10.1 General

- Company Shall determine and select opportunities for improvement any action to meet customer requirement and enhance satisfaction.
- These shall include – improving products and services to meet requirements and to address future needs and expectations correcting, preventing, or reducing undesirable effects, improving the performance and effectiveness of QMS.

10.2 Non-conformity and corrective actions

- Company shall react to the non-conformity take action to control and correct, deal with the consequences.
- Evaluate need for action to eliminate the cause so it does not recur and occur.
- Elsewhere. company shall review and analyze non-conformity, determine the cause, and determine similar non-conformity could exist

or potentially occur, implement action needed, review effectiveness of action taken.

- Update risk and opportunity during planning, make changes to QMS.
- Shall be appropriate to the non-conformity encountered.

Company shall retain documented information as evidence of nature of the non-conformity and any subsequent action taken and the results of any corrective action.

10.3 Continual Improvement

Company shall continually improve the suitability adequacy and effectiveness of the QMS.

Records related to clause 10

10.1

Company shall define opportunity for improvement indicated in MRM.

10.2

Company shall define procedure to handle non- conformity and corrective. actions

10.3

Company shall define continual improvement projects.

Clauses for documented information

4.3

Shall define scope of certification.

4.4.2

Shall define overall process flow chart and block diagram.

5.2.2

Shall define policy.

6.2.1

Shall define quality objectives.

7.1.5.1

Shall retain appropriate documented information as evidence of fitness for purpose of monitoring and measurement resources.

7.1.5.2

Basis used for calibration and verification shall be retained as documented. information

7.2

Retain documented information as evidence of competence.

7.5

Shall have details as per the entire clause Clauses for documented information.

8.1

Determine, maintain and retain documented information that process is carried out. as planned.

Demonstrate conformity of products and services

8.2.3.2

Shall retain documented information on the results of the review, on new. requirements of products and services

8.2.4

Shall ensure relevant documented information is amended and relevant people are made aware of the changed requirements.

8.3.2 to 8.3.6

Shall retain documented information for all the clauses indicated in the design and development process.

8.4.1

The company shall maintain documented information of these activities and actions arising from evaluations.

8.5.1

Availability of documented information that defines planning to post delivery. activity

8.5.2

Shall retain Documented information necessary to enable traceability.

8.5.3

Company Shall report loss or damage to customer and external provider and Shall retain Documented information on what has occurred.

8.5.6

Company Shall retain documented information describing the results of reviews and changes and action arising from the review.

8.6

Company Shall retain documented information on the release of products and services which shall include. Evidence of conformity with acceptance criteria, traceability of persons authorizing release

8.7.2

Company Shall retain documented information on describing the non-conformity, action taken, concessions obtained authority deciding the action in respect of non-conformity.

9.1.1

Company Shall retain documented information as evidence of the results of measurement and analysis.

9.2.2

Shall retain documented information as evidence of implementation of audit program and audit results

9.3.3

Company shall retain documented information as evidence of the results of management review output.

10.2.2

Company Shall retain documented information as evidence of nature of the non-conformity and any subsequent action taken and the results of any corrective action.

Management Involvement --Summary

- Define list of processes/sections and scope of certification, needs and expectation of an interesting party.
- Define Policy, roles and authority, approve Reporting system for each Process
- Define objectives, risk for process activity, and approve risk mitigation. Plan for each process
- Define list of resources, competency, and training communication system approve documentation for the ISO system and preservation norms.
- Establish service flow chart, control customer communication, , supplier management, work SOP and non-conforming services
- Define performance review for customer, suppliers and processes, audit frequency and auditors, Plan Management Review meeting.
- Define improvement opportunities, handle non-conformity, and take corrective actions

References

Abdul Kareem Mohamed Yasin, GDSCM. (2018). “AI Technologies Enhancing Supply Chain Management“. Retrieved from SIPMM: https://publication.sipmm.edu.sg/ai-technologies- enhancing-supply-chain-management, accessed 15/12/2019.

John Brownlee. (2019). “14 different type in machine learning”. Retrieved from https://machinelearningmastery.com/types-of-learning-in-machine-learning/,accessed 15/12/2019.

N.P. Singh, Ranjit Kumar and R.P. Singh, Agricultural Economics Research Review Vol. 19 (Conference No.) 2006 pp 23-36 Diversification of Indian Agriculture: Composition, Determinants and Trade Implications

Nillian Low, ADPSM. (2019).”Integrating IoT for effective supply chain“. Retrieved from SIPMM: https://publication.sipmm.edu.sg/integrating-ai-iot-effective-supply-chain, accessed 15/12/2019.

Sigfox.com. (2019). “IoT soil condition monitoring sensors will optimize agriculture through data”. Retrieved from https://www.sigfox.com/en/iot-soil-condition-monitoring-sensors- will-optimize-agriculture-through-data-2, accessed 15/12/2019.

Swetketu Trivedi. (2019). “How AI will change the retail industry?”. Retrieved from https://medium.com/datadriveninvestor/how-ai-will-change-the-retail-industry-in-2019-c817091c6306, accessed 15/12/2019.

United Nation.(2019). “The world population prospects 2019 Highlights”. Retrieved from https://population.un.org/wpp/Publications/Files/WPP2019_Highlights.pdf, accessed 15/12/2019.

Vaishnavi Putcha. (2019). “Role of Neurol Networks in Artificial Intelligence”. Retrieved from https://mindmajix.com/neural-network-in-artificial-intelligence, accessed 15/12/2019.